A Course in Miracles
In a Nutshell

Inspirational Messages
From the Heart

Book Two

A Course in Miracles In a Nutshell

Book Two

Inspirational Messages From the Heart

*"This is reality, and only this.
This is illusion's end.
It is the truth."*
- A Course in Miracles -

Francis M. "Bud" Morris

A Course in Miracles
In a Nutshell

Book Two
Inspirational Messages from the Heart

ISBN # 0-9777219-1-4

Copyright © 2006, Francis M. Morris. All rights reserved.

On the Internet at http://www.budmorris.com

Inquiries should be made to
Transformation Publications

Published by Transformation Publications
5529 E. Harmon Circle
Mesa, AZ 85215

Library of Congress Catalog Card Number 2006900528

Printed in USA through the publisher's agency, OPA Publishing
A division of Optimum Performance Associates
Box 1764
Chandler, AZ 85244-1764
E-mail: info@opapublishing.com
Online at: http://www.opapublishing.com

Table of Contents
Book Two

Table of Contents
Continued

Preface

Inspirational Messages from the Heart, Book Two in my series, A Course in Miracles – in a Nutshell, is a collection of articles that I have written, along with short pieces that have inspired me. This is indeed the representation of my highest joy—my writing and poetry—as manifested through me by Spirit. As I open myself to Spirit, my creative forces flow and I am startled with their clarity and completeness. I take credit only for having let go of my ego identification and joined with Spirit. When I drop the troubles of the world and go inside to hear the Voice for God, the work goes so much easier. The study of A Course in Miracles has enabled me to do this to a large extent, as well as reading metaphysical books, classes, teaching, and wonderful people in my life. A Course in Miracles is the inspiration for this book and for my life. I awaken sometimes at night with ideas and have often received inspiration during meditation. When I am ready, the writing writes itself. I am so blessed and am fully appreciative of every single one of the many learning opportunities that have enabled me to write this book.

I thank my wife, Peg Carter, and all of the inspiring teachers I have had through the years. I am deeply appreciative to the Agape International Center for Truth in Culver City, California and its minister, Rev. Dr. Michael Beckwith for all of the inspiration and blessings I received there. The same goes for Marianne Williamson; Rev. Dr. Kay Hunter at the Cathedral of Light in Carrollton, TX; Rev. Phyllis Clay Sparks at the Soul-Esteem Center in Maryland Heights, MO; and Rev. Dr. Michelle Medrano of the New Vision Center for Spiritual Growth in Scottsdale, AZ.

Finally, my grateful appreciation to Paul McNeese of OPA Publishing for his professional, dedicated and creative work on behalf of this and my other books. Acting as coach, mentor, business advisor and occasional editor, he led me through a maze of practical—yet easy-to-overlook—necessities and made the publishing of this book possible.

Introduction

This book should be looked upon as a transformational journey, but the trip is not linear. You may find yourself bouncing all over the place as you conscientiously follow the directions below. There is no step-by-step journey to follow, because everyone has a different path.

This book is dedicated to your spiritual growth and eventual transformation. It consists of many lessons for practical application in your everyday life. It is suggested that you read a section. Then, when you are ready, move to the next section.

Journal your thoughts, reactions, and feelings throughout each study period. Devote some time to meditation each day. Purchase *A Course in Miracles* and read above and below the Course quotes that follow each lesson. There are many Course quotes included, so this is, in fact, a rather deep study of the Course itself as well as a practical guide to living, as outlined in the lessons. Practice and think about the ideas in that section *conscientiously* for a period of time—long enough so that you feel you have absorbed all you can from the pages you are studying. There may be some sections with which you disagree; document your thoughts in the journal. There may be some that you do not completely understand. If so, don't get discouraged, just journal your thoughts and continue on with the lessons. Come back later to see if your understanding has changed.

Many aspects of spiritual growth are covered and this program will take time—you are worth that time. Your life and your joy are worth that time. This will help you to develop a spiritual practice, and developing a spiritual practice is vital. The time that it takes to do the required elements below are essential to your spiritual growth.

1. Read – Read a section and the quote or quotes that follow it. Think about them as you go through your day. Read the material again several times while you are on the lesson. If you have a particular need facing you, look through the Table of Contents and take an appropriate lesson instead, then come back to your original place.

2. Study – Contemplate the quotes from *A Course in Miracles* at the end of each section. Read the sections in the Course itself, and do not hesitate to read the Course material above and below the selected quotes as time allows (you can purchase the Course and the Course supplement *The Song of Prayer* through *http://www.miraclecenter.org/* or at your local metaphysical bookstore.).

3. Journal – Purchase a journal and journal each day. *See the following section in this book for help in journaling.* Many have found journaling to be an exceptionally valuable practice. Through journaling, you can look back two months or two years and see that what was going on in your life is not happening now—thus, you can see some progress in your spiritual growth and have hope for further growth. Use the following questions to prompt you in applying the journaling towards the lesson of the day.

> ➤ In what ways does the section specifically apply to your life?

> ➤ Discuss your successes/failures from your practice on the day before.

> ➤ What could you do to make things different today from yesterday or the day before?

> ➤ What attack thoughts/judgments have you had towards someone or something?

> ➤ How have your attitudes towards family, jobs, and world events changed?

Journal any further observations or feelings that might come to you, whether related to the lesson or not.

4. Meditate – Meditate daily for five to ten minutes; give that much time to Spirit and you will be amply rewarded. Find a quiet place, be still, and open your mind for spiritual guidance. Don't try to tell God anything or ask for special favors—just listen to your Higher Self. Purchase a musical CD/tape to help to deepen your meditations. There are many techniques; if you have problems, find a class to help you settle on the method that is right for you.

5. Ask for help – If you find challenges of any kind during your day, simply request clarification from Holy Spirit during your meditation. What healing purpose is there for you to experience in this person/event/situation? What lessons are you to learn from it? When/If you are truly willing to let it go, Spirit will be happy to take it from you! Remember that it takes time to put a situation in your life, so it could take time to be healed. Don't be in a hurry! We are not dealing with instant gratification in this book! Journal your experiences (see the following section—*Journaling*).

6. Join – Join some spiritual support group in your community if possible. Discussion groups are very valuable. If a group is not available, find a friend who has a sympathetic heart, who will listen to you without judging you or trying to "save" you. You could even start one—you don't have to be the "expert" to start a group—it could be a spiritual exploration group, or a spiritual book discussion. You could even form a journaling group centered on this material, sharing your breakthroughs on a weekly basis.

7. Continue your education – Go to a metaphysical bookstore for additional inspirational material.

Journaling

Many may not be aware of the importance and/or the techniques used in journaling. I call what we are doing here guided journaling, in that questions are provided to be addressed during the journaling process. However, this should not limit the journaling; cover those things that are staring you in the face day by day. Journal your feelings, thoughts, reactions, "high" times and "low" times.

Here are some journaling tips (from the informative website http://www.kporterfield.com/journal/Journal_Index.html):

> ➤ Look at a magazine and find a picture that appeals to you. Cut it out, paste it in your notebook and write about it.

> ➤ Draw a word portrait of your interior landscape. Next draw a word portrait of your exterior landscape.

> ➤ Write about an event in your life—first from your perspective and then from the perspective of someone else who was present.

> ➤ Write about a person or an event that is a paradox or contradiction.

> ➤ Turn a feeling—love, joy, beauty, anger or fatigue—into a character. Write a detailed description and dialog with this character.

> ➤ Write down everything that comes into your mind about money.

> ➤ Pick the first date from the past and place that pop into your mind. Now write a journal entry as though you were reliving a former lifetime.

> ➤ Write about a belief you've discarded.

> ➤ Your life is a journey. From where? To where? Write a travel article about this trip.

> ➤ Write an entry telling another person something that you are too afraid or reluctant to tell them.

Get into the habit of journaling regularly. Make sure that no one can access your journal so that you can express yourself freely and openly. You can try by just starting to write (without lifting your pen from the paper) anything that comes into your head. It doesn't have to make sense. Just write. Usually, after a while, things will start writing themselves. You will find the results of this kind of journaling very interesting.

Form your own style of journaling, though. It doesn't have to follow any guidelines. With an apology to Nike—Just do it!

What Is
A Course in Miracles?

Mention has been and will be made of *A Course in Miracles*. It is the basis of all my thinking, writing, and teaching. *A Course in Miracles* is a course of study that is read in many countries around the world, having been translated into nine languages, with several other translations in process. *A Course in Miracles* consists of three volumes: *The Text, The Workbook for Students*, and *The Manual for Teachers*. Most of the time, all three of these, in the above order, are contained in one volume. There are two versions of the Course. All quotes in this book are taken from the latest version.

The goal of the Course is the achievement of inner peace. The truth of the world is spiritual, and that which is spiritual cannot be seen with the eyes of the body. The truth is the presence of God, the peace of Christ, and the presence of the Holy Spirit in all situations and all people, whether or not that seems to be the case.

As you read *The Text*, there may be times when you don't understand what the Course is saying. When this happens, simply be patient and wait until you mature in the principles of the Course.

For example, The Text consistently speaks on two levels, that of man and that of God. Sometimes this becomes a little confusing. A study group would help with this issue—a list of study groups is also available from the Miracles Distribution Center. The Course is not to be intellectually analyzed. When you are ready to understand it, the teacher and the understanding will be there. If you have difficulty with a sentence or section, it will often be clarified in the next section.

I recommend that you start the study of the Course with the workbook, concentrating on one lesson per day. This involves reading the lesson in the morning and evening and keeping the thought with you all day long. The thought for the day is well used as the subject of meditation. Each lesson is very beautiful and transformative. The Preface is important—it relates the history of the origin of the Course. Also, the Introduction to and the 50 miracle principles at the beginning of The Text are valuable reading. Read in *The Text* and *Manual for Teachers* as you get the opportunity. The *Manual for Teachers* is not just for teachers—it is easy to read and clarifies terms and concepts in the Course. Everyone does the Course differently and the way they do it is perfect for them. There is no "right" way.

A Course in Miracles was channeled from Christ, providing an insight into Christ's love for God and for humankind and the source of his strength and miracles. In the Course, Christ urges you to remember your Father and your Father's Love for you. He tells you how much your Father needs you. He teaches you how to relate to the world, to your brother, and to yourself. He also redefines some biblical terms and concepts.

A Course in Miracles is a call to remember your Father, who loves you. It is alternatively simple, humorous, and complex. *The Text*, especially, is very profound and cannot be read like a novel—if you try, you will end up most confused! The authority from which the Course comes is apparent in every sentence. Christ's teaching techniques are without flaw, consistent, and totally beautiful. Quotes in this book are a mere sampling of the thousands of beautiful quotes in the Course.

A Course in Miracles approaches you and your fellow human being from a spiritual viewpoint. Both of you are extensions of your Father's Love, and as such, your basic nature is love. No matter what you may have done or been or what your brother may have done or been, your basic nature cannot be altered. The Course speaks of reality from the view of the spiritual nature of all things and all events. You learn through the Course to step back from the drama and trauma of the world to see, not through your physical eyes, but through your spiritual eyes, that your growth depends upon the growth of all of your brothers in God and vice-versa. As you see them you see yourself; as you treat them, you treat yourself. In them you find your salvation (healing). You learn how to form a different kind of relationship with all of humankind, with God, with Christ, and with yourself.

A Life Journey

"A life spent chasing other people's approval is a life spent on a pointless roller coaster of emotional high and lows, without ever knowing yourself."

— Rinnata Paries

I believe that all who choose to come into this world are here to work on certain spiritual issues. You have all the tools, the right parents, siblings, relatives, the right body; everything is in place for you to accomplish great spiritual growth. This is what the world is for. However, the world is a place that has a great tide of negativity, human suffering, resistance, and pain.

Early in life, alarming messages came from parent, sibling, or peer—that you are not enough, that you need something from somewhere, someone, or something to fulfill you. These are the ego's messages—the ego is a part of your mind that desires to keep you separate from your spiritual awareness. It would like you to believe that you are special and different, that you have different needs and different skills. However, the truth is that all Children of the One God were created equal. The ego is not outside of you, but is very much a subconscious urging, a voice in your mind that distracts you from your search for God. The ego is very real, tempting you in many and varied ways from your path and your original goals. The ego lures you with drugs, sex, excitement, body worship, gluttony, alcohol, and many others, all of which are "gods" to replace the one true God.

This results in what *A Course in Miracles* calls a split mind. You are torn asunder, going around in circles and cycles, going against the flow, swimming upstream, confused, lost, in pain, depressed, in despair, all the time searching desperately outside of yourself for happiness and fulfillment. These provide the obstacles that you meet which you have the opportunity to use to make you stronger. All the time that the ego is taking you on a tour of these "treasures" of the world, you are still motivated by your original desire for God. You see, it is a paradox! The journey on which the ego attempts to lead you helps you to accomplish your spiritual path; the ego doesn't know this—it is very shortsighted.

The journey on which the Holy Spirit would lead you is filled with love, joy, peace, and fulfillment. Constantly remind yourself that when you are in pain, you are following your ego's belief system and when you are joyful, you are following the Holy Spirit's belief system. The two are mutually exclusive.

There is no need to learn through pain. And gentle lessons are acquired joyously, and are remembered gladly. What gives you happiness you want to learn and not forget. ... You are not a happy learner yet because you still remain uncertain that vision gives you more than judgment does, and you have learned that both you cannot have.

Text, pg. 446

Glory is God's gift to you, because that is what He is. See the glory everywhere to remember what you are.

Text, pg. 143

Truth cannot deal with errors that you want.

Text, pg. 43

The way to God is through forgiveness here. There is no other way.

Workbook, p22

Feel the Glory

Our birth is but a sleep and a forgetting. The soul that rises with us, our life's star, hath had elsewhere its setting, and comet from afar: not in entire forgetfulness, and not in utter nakedness, but trailing clouds of glory do we come from God, who is our home.

- William Wordsworth

Those who experience a near death experience report seeing, among other things, a tunnel, at the end of which is a bright light. It occurs to me that the tunnel is actually leading inward, rather than outward; the bright light is Spirit Within that has been there all along. You can experience this without all the trappings by just quieting your mind, letting go of all expectations and control, and going to the deepest part of you. You are infinite within and there is an infinity outside of you. Your job is to minimize the separation between the two (the ego), allowing a constant flow to occur and to experience joy and peace and love as part of your physical experience. Be still and know that Thou art God also. Be still, and claim your god-given Power, Wisdom and the infinite presence that you are . . . now!

Feel the Glory
Feel the Beauty
Feel the Glory deep inside

- John Astin

Feel the Glory as you dance and play and work. Feel the Beauty as you look in the mirror. Feel the Glory deep inside—you are a glorious and unique creation of God.

Spirit am I, a holy Son of God, free of all sins, safe and healed and whole; free to forgive, and free to save the world."

Text, pg. 173

The Valley
Of the Shadow

"No death can come unto the soul of man
Though paths may wind through darkest gloom,
For God is Life and you are life, and life
And Life are one."
- Ernest & Fenwicke Holmes, *The Voice Celestial*

Yea, when you are walking through the valley of the shadow of death, pain, and taxes, fear no evil! God has given you a Comforter—the Holy Spirit. Give Him your troubles, your pain, your fears. Release to Him your problems and your troubled relationships. He will take them from you—but first you must completely release them. The shadow of death is simply a place where the Light of God is behind a cloud—there is no death. You are Spirit and have eternal life!

Come to me, O fearful and troubled ones.
Come to me and let me soothe your fears.
Come to me with open hands and hearts,
Releasing to me your deepest fears.
There is no sickness that cannot be healed,
There is no sinner that cannot be saved from himself,
There is no madness that cannot be lifted,
There is no lack that cannot be fulfilled,
There is no darkness that cannot be lit.
I am ever here, ever loving you, for I am deep within you.
So come to me, now, this moment,
Bring your heavy-laden heart to me,
And allow me to connect you to your Higher Self -
Your Holy Father, Who is lost in your darkness.
Turn from the darkness, into the Light -
The Light of Love, which is your Truth.

—Bud Morris

Our Father, bless our eyes today. We are Your messengers, and we would look upon the glorious reflections of Your Love which shines in everything. We live and move in You alone. We are not separate from Your Eternal Life. There is no death, for death is not Your Will. And we abide where You have placed us, in the life we share with You and with all living things, to be like You and part of You forever. We accept Your Thoughts as ours, and our will is one with Yours eternally. Amen.

Workbook, pg. 310

As forgiveness allow love to return to my awareness, I will se a world of peace and safety and joy.

Workbook, pg. 90

When you are afraid, be still and know that god is real, and you are His beloved Son in whom He is well pleased.

Text, pg. 55

On the Devil's Trampoline?

Evil, and evil spirits, devils and devil possession, are the outgrowth of man's inadequate consciousness of God. We must avoid thinking of evil as a thing in itself-a force that works against man or, against God, if you will.

- Eric Butterworth

Are you on the devil's trampoline? Up and down? Sad and happy? Angry and joyful? Playful and tragic? I don't believe in the devil, but I have been very familiar with the trampoline of life.

The ego delights in your constant play of emotions and the resulting confusion. He would have you focus on the bottom of the tapestry of life, where all its threads are hanging and confused, rather than the beautiful picture on the top of the tapestry. Be very sure that you are very much at its beckon call when you allow your emotions to control your life. I don't denigrate emotions as such. Feel your feelings, but don't let them run you. If you bury your feelings they will end up having symptoms such as cancer and other diseases.

Live your life in such a way that you recognize the point at which the feelings exceed a certain point between sad and happy, for instance. Take the middle road. You are a thought in the Mind of God. Your notes add resonance, harmony and beauty to the Song of the Universe.

Beyond the body, beyond the sun and stars, past everything you see and yet somehow familiar, is an arc of golden light that stretches as you look into a great and shining circle. And all the circle fills with light before your eyes. The edges of the circle disappear, and what is in it is no longer contained at all. The light expands and covers everything, extending to infinity forever shining and with no break or limit anywhere.

Text, pg. 447

Competition

"The only competition worthy a wise man is with himself."

- Anna Brownell Jameson

Competition is about getting ahead of your brother, getting somewhere first, winning, making him lose, or not losing yourself. The win-win situation calls for *each* person being a winner. It calls for you to not put the other person down, and to work together for the highest and best of all concerned. The Holy Spirit, however, works through stimulating oneness, and focuses on similarities. People are like crabs in a basket. When one gets close to getting out, one that is trying to climb over pulls it back down.

Competition calls for attack. The ego works through judgment, attack, and separation—separating you from your brother. Have you noticed the driver who races down the road or cuts you off just for the privilege of being first at the stoplight? How about the politician who attacks his opponent in many ways?

The western world is much given to competition in business, in sports, in universities, in families. Take games like professional football, where the losers and winners mingle after the game and salute each other, sometimes even pray with one another. This is competition on a higher level. In business, for example, when two people are competing for a sale and they do so with integrity and a cheerful heart, there is no loser. If the one who "lost" simply goes on and finds another opportunity for a sale, supported by the good wishes of the one who won. If he grouses around and complains about the unfairness of the world, then he makes himself a loser. If the one who "wins" flaunts his victory in the other's face, and put him down then he becomes a loser in spite of his victory.

There is no winner and no loser in Spirit. We play the game and however it comes out is the way it should be and the way it is. There is no gain in regretting past games, only in learning from them. When you can do this, you win.

Who can attack the Son of God and not attack his Father? How can God's Son be weak and frail and easily destroyed unless his Father is? You do not see that every sin and every condemnation that you perceive and justify is an attack upon your Father. And that is why it has not happened, nor could be real. You do not see that this is your attempt because you think the Father and the Son are separate. And you must think that They are separate, because of fear. For it seems safer to attack another or yourself than to attack the great Creator of the universe, Whose power you know.

Text, pg. 483

Do you prefer that you be right or happy?

Text, pg. 617

Let us ascend together to the Father, by giving Him ascendance in our minds.

Text, pg. 361

I Rest in God Today

"I rest in God today, and let Him work in me and through me, while I rest in Him in quiet and in perfect certainty."

- Workbook, pg. 213

Lesson 94 from the Course Workbook says it all: You are as God created you—in the love, in the light, in the glory—you are His Son eternally. There is nothing you need do to get better—you are perfect right now. There is nothing you can do to return to God's Love because you never really left. There is no need to get out of hell—you were never there.

The most graphic description of the fear of hell comes from the movie *Ghost*, when the bad guy dies and the spirit comes out of his body only to be taken away to hell by ugly, screaming terrors from the underworld. I get the feeling of fear that the Bible is out to give me when I see that movie. However, I know that God loves His children—that God did not create a hell and would not send them to such a place to burn to eternity. I cannot say for sure what happens when we die, but I believe that God will be gracious and loving to me, offering me another life somewhere to try to get it right.

You are not a sinner; you have never sinned! Lay aside all idols and self-images, both "good" and "bad, they are ego's playground. Reclaim your inheritance and your power. You are not and never could be a victim of anything in this world; you are as God created you.

...when any situation arises which tempts you to become disturbed, say "There is another way of looking at this."

Workbook, pg. 50

Living Life

"Experience is a hard teacher.
First comes the test, then the lesson."

- Vernon Sanders' Law

Billions of people out there think that they know how to live life. They fritter their lives away searching in vain for happiness, peace, joy and love. Even when they think they have found happiness, peace, joy or love, they are often disappointed because that euphoric feeling is only temporary. They, for the most part, are searching for these qualities in all the wrong places, in the wrong people, in the wrong way. *If* their husband/wife/boyfriend/girlfriend would understand them they would be happy. *If* they had a million dollars they would be happy. *If* their job didn't demand so much time they would be happy. *If* their boss were nicer to them they would be happy.

They dwell either in regret for the past or in fear of the future, seldom in the present. They search for completion, they search for help, they search for a "soul mate," and they search for power. They already have power and help, and they can be their *own* soul mate. They search for something that does not exist outside them. They are truly lost because they have not made the gross realization that their greatest gifts are given to themselves.

Do these things fit any part of your life? The good news is that *your* happiness (and theirs) does not lie in someone else! If it did, you would be a puppet! It is an inside job. When Jesus said that ye are Gods, he wasn't just saying words that sounded good. He was giving us the secret to how to live our lives—from the inside out. Start from within. Search within. *All that you need is within you.* There is a universe within, as well as without. The goal is to allow that spiritual nature that is within you to flow freely outward. The lighter and more permeable you become, the more the spirit flows.

Take responsibility for your life. Don't blame other people or situations. Don't blame God or your spouse. Don't blame "them"—"they" made me do it. And don't think you are hiding your mistakes of the past. God is not mocked. Acknowledge them and get on with your life. Forgive others whom you have blamed

10

in the past; forgive yourself for your errors in thinking. Let go and let God use you as His instrument in healing the world.

Happiness is connecting to your Source—to God. He will wipe your tears away. He is the abundant center of all Life. His Life is your life that flows in your blood, that life which lies deep within every cell of your body. His Breath gave you your life. Be thankful for all the blessings that your have had, that you have right now, and that you will have in the future. That is the secret for living life and living it abundantly.

If your brothers are part of you and you blame them for your deprivation, you are blaming yourself. And you cannot blame yourself without blaming them. That is why blame must be undone, not seen elsewhere. Lay it to yourself and you cannot know yourself, for only the ego blames at all. Self-blame is therefore ego identification, and as much an ego defense as blaming others. You cannot enter God's Presence if you attack His Son. When His Son lifts his voice in praise of his Creator, he will hear the Voice for his Father. Yet the Creator cannot be praised without His Son, for Their glory is shared and They are glorified together.

Text, pg. 201

It's Not My Responsibility!

One's philosophy is not best expressed in words; it is expressed in the choices one makes. In the long run, we shape our lives and we shape ourselves. The process never ends until we die. And, the choices we make are ultimately our own responsibility.

- Eleanor Roosevelt

There are many people who, when they hear the dire predictions about the future of this society, culture, and planet, deny any responsibility. Not only that, but they deny that they can help solve the dilemma in which we find ourselves.

➤ We are killing species by the thousands
➤ We have created a hole in the ozone
➤ We are experiencing global warming
➤ We are destroying the rain forests in Brazil and elsewhere
➤ We are polluting the rivers, lakes, and oceans
➤ We have more and more violent children
➤ Our prisons are filled to overflowing
➤ We are experiencing a wild fluctuation of the temperature, weather, and earth—hurricanes, tornadoes, floods, droughts, earthquakes
➤ Prejudice against others still exists
➤ Families are missing father or mother or both with increasing regularity
➤ Drugs are consumed at all levels of society
➤ Parents don't know how to raise (discipline) their children
➤ Many churches exacerbate these conditions by promoting more prejudice and guilt in their flocks
➤ . . . and so on

The problems "out there" seem just too big and too many or too all encompassing to be faced by the average person. They feel increasingly a victim to circumstances rather than as being in any way responsible. They say such things as; "They did it", or "They should . . ." or "There ought to be a law . . ." or "What can only one man do?" The problems seem to be outside them—in other people, in the ghettoes, or in other countries—never in them. "How could the loss of rainforests, for example, be my fault?"" How can I solve the problem of pollution or crime or drugs or violent children?"

They (we) (I) must realize that they (we) (I) participate in the formation of group thought in this world. (Group thought is the sum of the thinking of mankind that influences the individual mind.) Every violent thought—even those unexpressed—contributes to crime, to violence exhibited by children, and to road rage, etc. When you have a thought of lust, that is, an inordinate craving for the pleasures of the body, you contribute to sexual deviation, rape, and sexual abuse of all sorts. Everything you say is a demand upon the Universe. Many of your problems originate in your thinking. You have thousands of thoughts every day. Be aware of them and their effect upon you and others. Responsibility does not imply guilt. **A Course in Miracles** tells you to not seek to change the world, but merely to change your thinking about the world. You can help, but do not get caught up in the insanity of the world. See the highest and best for all. Feel compassion for those in pain.

You might tend to be judgmental of qualities in yourself that you deem to be "bad," while someone else may have an entirely different opinion. Both of your opinions come from your past, and they are only opinions. The past is gone! Give yourself some slack! You might admire a certain quality that someone else possesses and wish that you could have it also. Only your thinking and your decision keep you from doing this. If you like and admire the quality, it doesn't matter what someone else thinks! You can recreate yourself any time that you desire to do so.

When you look into the mirror, do you see only one person standing there and lament, "What can I do?" Christ was *only* one person! Gandhi was *only* one person. Buddha, Martin Luther King, Jr., and Mother Teresa were all *only* one person. Look what they accomplished. You are not being asked to necessarily go to the extreme that they did, but you can find peace within your heart and express it through your actions. You most effectively teach peace to others by being peaceful. Teach peace everywhere you go, for that is what you truly are. Demonstrate peace by being peaceful in all your relationships and in your thoughts.

How can you who are so holy suffer? All your past except its beauty is gone, and nothing is left but a blessing. I have saved all your kindnesses and every loving thought you ever had. I have purified them of the errors that hid their light, and kept them for you in their own perfect radiance. They are beyond destruction and beyond guilt. They came from the Holy Spirit within you, and we know what God creates is eternal. You can indeed depart in peace because I have loved you as I loved myself.
You go with my blessing and for my blessing.

Text, pg. 83

I am responsible for what I see. I choose the feelings that I experience, and I decide upon the goal I would achieve. And everything that seems to happen to me I ask for, and receive as I have asked.

Text, pg. 448

Lord, Make Me
An Instrument
Of Your Peace

"The moving finger writes, and having writ,
Moves on; nor all your Piety nor Wit
Shall lure it back to cancel half a line,
Nor all your Tears wash out a word of it."

- Omar Khyam, *Rubàyàt*

Lord, make me an instrument of Your Peace.

God may not use you as you expect to be used or as you want to be used, necessarily. God's Love can be expressed in many ways. Meditate upon your intuitions, your feelings and follow your intuitions if your meditations around them feel good and right and helpful to all concerned. The voice of the ego is loudest. Listen for the still, small voice. The path through following your intuition may not be as expected, but there is always a blessing. You can find peace wherever you are, no matter the circumstances, because the peace is within and never can be lost.

Where there is hatred, let me sow Love.

Hatred comes in many forms—prejudices based upon race, religion, origin, judgments, holding grudges, getting even, refusing to talk to or acknowledge someone, avoiding contact with someone, and myriad other ways. Even if your feelings arise from events from years and years ago, you can practice daily—minute by minute—to erase them from your consciousness.

Where there is injury, let me sow Pardon.

Commit to being more gentle and kind in your dealings with all, to allow people to cut in front of you in traffic, to see when a waitress has too many tables to wait on each one properly, to see the worker who does poor work as not a "bad" person. Find a way to let these feelings go and to treat others in the way you would like to be treated.

Where there is discord, let me sow Unity.

Discord comes from being in traffic, from the busy-ness and rushes of the day, from competition to be first or to be the best, from seeing yourself as having to be right rather than happy. From discord comes a disharmony that brings a deep underlying dissatisfaction with life in general. Recognize God—the Unity—minute by minute. Maintain contact with Him. Ask Him to help you through and rise above these conditions.

Where there is doubt, let me sow Faith.

Having doubt in your own strength is a reflection on the Power that created you. You are made in the likeness and image of God in your spiritual nature.

Where there is error, let me sow Truth.

Many people label errors as "sins". They don't realize that it is a natural thing to make errors when you forget who you really are. They have forgotten. Their "sins" are forgiven them by God—God never recognized them in the first place. Can you not do so as well? All are children of God, unique expressions of Spirit in a physical form. He who "sins" against you is your best teacher, to be thanked, for he is showing you where healing is needed in yourself.

Where there is despair, let me sow Hope.

Despair is related to depression. Both are anger that is directed within, seeing a lack or limitation therein. Be still and know that you are God in expression, glorious and filled with all the wondrous qualities of the Christ. Stand tall and let your light shine, knowing that you live in a perfect universe, and that the universe is there to support you in every way. Remember that where a door or a window closes, another one is opened.

Where there is sadness, let me sow Joy.

Joy is lightness in the heart, a soaring, floating feeling that makes the day easier and the pathway straighter. Joy is gladness, and those who are sad have lost touch with joy. Sadness often is concentrated towards a seemingly hopeless future, or a painful past. Live in the moment and let the past and future go and you teach others by your example. Sow seeds of joy and happiness and they return to you multiplied. Somehow, sometime, those seeds catch hold and grow roots where it seemed least likely to happen.

Where there is darkness, let me sow Light.

Light is life and understanding. Darkness is fear, and fear flees at the light of truth. Darkness is separation from God and separation from God is impossible. The ego demands separation. The ego thrives in the darkness and dies in the light. While walking through the valley of the shadow of darkness, fear no evil. You are sustained and maintained by the most powerful force in the universe.

Oh, divine Master, grant that I may not so much seek to be consoled as to console,

Often, what we say is not nearly as important as just being still and knowing the Truth. A tender smile, a tear, and a shoulder to cry on provide much consolation and compassion.

To be understood as to understand,

See beyond the physical to the beauty underneath. Understand that everyone who attacks you is expressing a call for love. Separate the person from the act. A child who fails is readily forgiven because he does not yet know a lot of things about life and the way things work. An adult who fails is blamed for his stupidity; he is judged as a "sinner." He has simply forgotten who he really is. He is lost because you have judged him and locked him in a prison. Release him in your mind and your thinking.

To be loved as to love.

Still your heart, let go your hands, roll back the stone. Release the chains that lock your heart. Free yourself from the prison house of envy, fear, anger, and despair. Open your heart and send your love forth to all.

For it is in giving that we receive.

Give without concern for return. Give freely, without expectations simply because it is your nature. That is the way the universe works. The rivers and streams that flow freely are filled with life and growth. Those that are blocked by fear, greed, and hoarding become stagnant.

It is in pardoning that we are pardoned.

Forgiveness heals retroactively, back to the time of the original pain. Being forgiving blesses. Being unforgiving poisons. It is as though you swallowed poison and expected someone else to die.

There is only one of us—one of us in many forms, colors, religions, beliefs, activities, preferences—allow forgiveness to happen instantly when you become aware of the slightest tinge of hatred. Love your neighbor as you wish to be loved.

It is in dying that we are born to eternal life.

There is no death. The Son of God is free! Christ came here to demonstrate this for you. Fear not death. There is only one life, the Life of God, the Life everlasting. The living weep not for the dead but for themselves. They weep for their own loss, for their fear of death, of the unknown. The vehicle has been left behind while the Spirit, freed of this constriction, flies freely once more.

- St. Francis of Assisi

If you want peace you must abandon the teacher of attack.
The Teacher of peace will never abandon you.

Text, pg. 299

God knows you only in peace, and this is your reality.

Text, pg. 4

This Is the Day

"This is the day that God hath made.
Let us be glad and rejoice in it."

- Psalm 118:24

Do you wake up, get dressed, eat breakfast, get in the car, arrive at work, work, go to meetings, go to lunch, go to meetings, go back to the car, arrive at home, greet the wife/husband/kids/pets, read the paper, eat supper, watch the news, watch TV programs or read, and go to bed without once thinking of God, without once paying attention to the spiritual part of you, without remembering what the day is actually for? Not until you get to church—if you attend church?

What *is* the day actually for? It is for teaching and learning things of God—not that I have anything against being in business or whatever you do during the work hours, as long as you realize that whatever you do during those work hours is not about making a living. God gives you your life. God *is* your life. He is the substance of everything in your life. I realize, of course, that you require food and clothes and transportation in this modern age. But, as the Christ said, be *in* the world but not *of* it. Render under Caesar that which is Caesar's, but at the same time, dedicate your life to God. Let Him guide you. Let Him be your Source, your paymaster, your personal uplifter.

How many miracles do you have the opportunity to do each day that you miss because you are "disengaged"? How many miracles do you have happen around you each day that you miss for the same reason? How many wondrous sunsets and sunrises go unnoticed? How many people have come to you for help that you have passed by? How many times in the slow rush hour do you grumble at the traffic rather than spending time being thankful and appreciative of all your blessings? How much negative energy do you build up during the day, to be redistributed to others at work or to those at home?

Father, I thank You for today, and for the freedom I am certain it will bring. This day is holy, for today Your Son will be redeemed. His suffering is done. For he will hear Your Voice directing him to find Christ's vision through forgiveness, and be free forever from all suffering. Thanks for today, my Father. I was born into this world but to achieve this day, and what it holds in joy and freedom for Your holy Son and for the world he made, which is released along with him today.

Workbook, pg. 472

I place the peace of God in your heart and in your hand, to hold and to share. The heart is pure to hold it, and the has are strong to give it. We cannot lose.

Text, pg. 83

You will find heaven. Everything you seek but this will fall away.

Workbook, pg. 239

To be in the Kingdom is merely to focus your full attention on it.

Text, pg. 117

Innocence

"Children are generally happy because they don't yet have a file in their minds called "All the Things That Could Go Wrong." They don't have a mind-set that puts "Things to Fear" before "Things to Love." Unless we can be like little children, we can't enter into the kingdom of heaven; unless we can be like little children, we can't be happy. Children are happy because they don't have all the facts yet."

- Marianne Williamson, *Illuminata*

Return to innocence. Become as a child; that is, recognize your innocence. Recognize that you were created and still maintain your essential innocence. Drop your walls of sophistication and specialness. No one but you can show you the way you need to go. Seek not for gurus, but for the leadership of the Holy Spirit. Find the loving and guiltless Self inside of you that never was and never could be corrupted. Follow this Self in perfect innocence. You *are* in this world of complexity, but strive to keep in mind, as you go from task to task, that your basic nature is purity and innocence. Innocence does not judge. In this realization, forget this world, and come with wholly empty hands unto your God. In your innocence is your power. When you don't use your mind to manipulate or have preconceptions of how things should be, when you are open to God's Will, then you inherit your kingdom; then you find true power.

You are a divine Child of God, who never really left God because that which God created is part of Him and could never leave its Source. When God created you, He extended His nature to you. You are not a sinner because God could not create something that is not part of His nature. That which was true at your creation is true for you now and is also true of every other person that is, was, or ever will be! Be kind and loving at every opportunity and bless your brother for his illusions, and know that God has already forgiven you for yours.

But the content of the course never changes. Its central theme is always, "God's Son is guiltless, and in his innocence is his salvation."

Manual for Teachers, pg. 3

"Except you become as little children" means that unless you fully recognize your complete dependence on God, you cannot know the real power of the Son in his true relationship with the Father.

Text, pg. 12

In you is all of Heaven. Every leaf that falls is given life in you. Each bird that ever sang will sing again in you. And very flower that ever bloomed has saved its perfume and its loveliness for you.

Text, pg. 527

God's Son is guiltless, and in his innocence is his salvation.

Manual for Teachers, pg. 3

Abundance

"The poor will always be among us—they are the ones who haven't recognized the truth of who they are, haven't opened up themselves to infinite supply."

- *The Science of Mind* Text—What It Does

Abundance is humankind's inheritance from the Creator. All that you desire is yours so long as it does not hurt anyone else and you do not step on your supply lines. Stepping on the supply line stops the flow—that can happen many ways. When you as a Son of God deny your inheritance, put idols in God's place, or inhibit the natural flow of goodness in any way, you are denying the Presence of God within you and are stopping your good.

Abundance is very much related to tithing—you have to prime a pump before it starts giving water out of the ground. The tree has its roots in the ground, but does not suck at the earth. It creates a vacuum condition that makes room for more fluid/nutrients to flow from the earth. It is not your job to get—to claw and scheme to fill your bank accounts. It is your job to simply receive.

Abundance for me has been a wonderful experience. A few years ago, my income just didn't seem to keep up with the bills. I had to manipulate, pay bills late, and still came up short. I would wake in the middle of the night with nightmares of having to declare bankruptcy. I believe that two of my marriages failed partially as a result of this anxiety. One of my recurring fears was of growing old and feeble, eating dog food because I couldn't afford anything else. Finally, I realized, as abundance lecturer Edwene Gaines says, "Debtors can't eat me." I finally realized that bankruptcy wasn't the worst thing that could happen to me—it was of a lesser "badness" than the fear and anxiety that I had been going through. As a result, I never had to declare bankruptcy. These realizations enabled me to let go of the fear and anxiety. I started tithing and have found a peace of mind around money and savings that I had never experienced before. The money I need shows up from unexpected places. I don't have to worry (worry is counter-productive, anyway). What a wonderful release!

What you are really wanting when you ask for a new car, for example, is the spiritual quality behind the car for which you are asking—happiness and joy. In other words, if you are asking for more income so you can pay your bills, you are requesting the Abundance of God to take that form. If you are asking for a happy relationship in your life, you are requesting the Love of God to take that form. This is spiritual malpractice! Seek ye *first* the Kingdom of Heaven, and all else will follow. You will be happy; you will be fed; you will be clothed; your bills will be paid. And when you are ready, the perfect relationship will show up. When it was said that all else would follow, almost everyone says "Yeah, right! Maybe someone special, like Donald Trump or Bill Gates, but not me!" Why not you? You deserve it! You are searching for the worldly by-product of the God-essence and skipping over the fact that you already have that essence to start with. Don't focus on the dollar and bills owed. It narrows your vision. Wealth has nothing to do with salary and everything to do with spiritual substance. It came with you when you were born. It was part of the package! When you make this connection real in your consciousness, God's "goodies" are drawn to you without effort.

You are complete and always have been. Remember your true nature, because the truth never changes; it always is true, no matter how it looks to the physical eyes. When you make that realization, when you connect with that truth in you, all you will have to do is accept what the world offers you and that will reflect that which you have connected with on the inside, that which you have realized—"made real." This is very important. Seek not outside yourself, for you will be sadly disappointed every time. If you bring a thimble to the Universe to be filled, it will be filled. Whether you bring a large bucket or a tanker truck, they will be filled. The size and shape of the bowl is your choice, based on your internal realization of your true nature, and, coming from your true nature, will never cause loss or pain to someone else.

This is a feast unlike indeed to those the dreaming of the world has shown. For here, the more that anyone receives, the more is left for all the rest to share. The Guests have brought unlimited supply with Them. And no one is

deprived or can deprive. Here is a feast the Father lays before His Son, and shares it equally with him. And in Their sharing there can be no gap in which abundance falters and grows thin. Here can the lean years enter not, for time waits not upon this feast, which has no end. For love has set its table in the space that seemed to keep your Guests apart from you.

Text, pg. 597

Only you can deprive yourself of anything. Do not oppose this realization, for it is truly the beginning of the dawn of light.

Text, pg. 201

The cost of giving is receiving.

Text, pg. 275

Work with Love

"Work is love made visible.
And if you cannot work with love but only with distaste,
it is better that you should leave your work and sit
at the gate of the temple
and take alms of those who work with joy.
For if you make bread with indifference, you bake a bitter bread
that feeds but half man's hunger.
And if you grudge the crushing of the grapes,
your grudge distills a poison in the wine.
And if you sing though as angels, and love not the singing,
you muffle man's ears to the voices of the day and
the voices of the night."

- Kahlil Gibran, *The Prophet*

The quote above is a highly romantic and exceedingly poetic way of describing work done well, yet is very true. Work is something for which many of you are looking. Work is something that many of you are resisting. Work is something that many of you do quite well, but without joy. Work is often seen as a "have-to" in this world of doing. As American singer Margaret Young once pointed out, "*Often people attempt to live their lives backwards; they try to have more things more money, in order to do more of what they want, so they will be happier. The way it actually works is the reverse. You must first be who you really are, then do what you need to do in order to have what you want.*"

With this thought in mind, view the idea of work with the understanding that you are in the perfect place at *all* times! You might be in the place for your own growth, or to be the light, or for someone else's growth. You cannot judge why you are there, but you can do whatever work is assigned to you to the very best of your ability, finding joy from within yourself and appreciation for yourself through work done well.

When work is performed with enthusiasm, love, and joy, it changes the atmosphere of the workplace. It changes the attitude of the supervisor and the coworkers towards you. If you are being abused in a position, staying is not recommended. When your purpose there is complete, the job will be complete and another will be waiting for you. You will know from within yourself the completion. Go without fear to the next. You might even change your mind and find a position within the company that suits you more appropriately, with more money and a step up the corporate ladder.

All things work together for good.

Text, pg. 65

Beware of the temptation to perceive yourself unfairly treated.

Text, pg. 563

We Are All One

A miracle is nothing more or less than this. Anyone who has come into a knowledge of his true identity, of his oneness with the all-pervading wisdom and power, this makes it possible for laws higher than the ordinary mind knows of to be revealed to him.

- Ralph Waldo Trine

What you are expresses so loudly that people can't hear a word you speak. It roars from your actions, from your vibratory system and everyone around you "gets it." They hear what you think you are trying to hide. We are all one. There is no hiding who you are; your children follow the example you set. Your deepest fears are expressed in one way or another. Your wife/husband know how you truly feel about them at some level. Clean up your act by practicing the presence of God moment by moment. Let go of situations and people that are not in integrity with your highest good. Let go, little by little, of judgments of others, of judgments of yourself, of addictions and ego thoughts. As you empty yourself of these things and simultaneously open the door to God, all the Good of life rushes in. Ask Holy Spirit to take these things because you don't need the pain and guilt any more. Find inspiration in all life around you every day.

Allow yourself to see your greatness, your beauty which has no equal in all the earth. You are a unique Child of God, in whom God is well pleased. As you do, you will be healed of your burdens. Miracles will come from directions unexpected. You will experience greater joy than you ever have before, more fun than you ever have before. You will see life differently, you will see people differently, you will see *yourself* differently, you will see your work differently, your family, and your home differently. And as you allow that small possibility that things could be not so bad, not so awful, not so terrible, you become open to the idea that God works through *all* things great and small to create His miracles. Rejoice in each day that comes up, know that it is the day that God has made to give you an opportunity to learn anew of yourself, to change your perceptions about life, and to be more aware of the miracle in living for God and you will be teaching love rather than fear.

It is impossible to overestimate your brother's value.

Text, pg. 434

God's Son is One. Whom God has joined as one, the ego cannot put asunder.

Text, pg. 356

You are being blessed by every beneficent thought of any of your brothers anywhere.

Text, pg. 72

It is impossible to remember God in secret and alone. For remembering Him means you are not alone, and are willing to remember it.

Text, pg. 295

Pray without Ceasing

I pray without ceasing now. My personal prayer is: Make me an instrument which only truth can speak.

- Peace Pilgrim

How often do you bring work home, only to ignore your children/wife, creating more strife and stress around you? Why then do you wonder why things are not harmonious at work or home? How fast does your life go? Are you having fun? Are you giving back to life as much as you can towards what you got? How much joy do you experience each minute of each day?

You *can* experience joy each minute. You *can* "pray without ceasing." You *can* stay in contact with God regardless of what is going on in your life. It takes practice and dedication to set aside a part of you to keeping that pipeline open, that communication going. Be open and aware of the Life of God expressing in and around you. Listen to the Joy of God expressing through the birds. See the Beauty of God expressing through the sunsets and sunrises daily. Feel the Love of God through your pets— unconditional love. Allow this Joy and this Life and this Beauty and this Love to fill you to bursting right now. Let it erase any pain, fear and doubt, disease or lack and limitation that you may have felt before this moment.

God is not about boredom. Heaven is not a place where nothing happens. Heaven is trying to express through you right now—in your home, in your car, in your place of work, in your church. There is excitement there, the excitement of change, the excitement of growth, the excitement of finding a new way of experiencing and passing on God's Love to others.

There will still be days when "stuff" happens. These become reduced to hours and are further reduced to minutes. You will find yourself having to go into meditation to feel God's Bliss more often. You will have shorter periods of turmoil and anxiety and longer periods of peace. You will find you have shorter periods of "highs" and longer periods of peace. But in this peace that becomes so much more prevalent, you do not lose *you*. Your identity and personality do not become merged into a meaningless void. You become more of who you truly are. Your personality becomes more vibrant, more dynamic and robust. You will find that people will love to be around you, to experience your vibrant self. That peace that passeth all understanding will flow from you as from a river to all around you and you will draw peaceful things and situations unto you. "Bad" things will find some other place to happen because you don't accept them any more.

And prayer is as continual as life. Everyone prays without ceasing. Ask and you have received, for you have established what it is you want.

Song of Prayer, pg. S-1.II.2

If you cannot hear the Voice for God, it is because you do not choose to listen.

Text, pg. 62

The Holy Spirit will direct you only so as to avoid pain. Surely no one would object to this goal if he recognized it. The problem is not whether what the Holy Spirit says is true, but whether you want to listen to what He says.

Text, pg. 134

No one who truly seeks the peace of God can fail to find it.

Workbook, pg. 350

Mastership

"...continually remind yourself that when you are dealing with the creative process, you are talking abut the working of a mind in a vertical or intuitive perception, an infinite potential for unfoldment that works from within you like a fountain."

— Eric Butterworth, *The Creative Life*

What if you lived your life as the Master of all you survey? You can change your thinking and change your life—in an instant! Think of it. You can be at choice instead of a victim of the thinking of the world. Here is the formula:

Rise above the petty judging of others. It is not your role in life to be the judge of others. You do not know enough to judge anyone.

Rise above the petty judgments that others make of you. You do not need to be swayed by what others think of you. Remain centered in your knowledge of who you are as a Child of God. If someone doesn't like you or treats you unkindly it is simply a call for love. That doesn't necessarily mean to try to get close to them, but to simply see beyond their façade to the Child of God they truly are.

Treat yourself and your past with love and kindness. You, also, are a Divine Child of God. You, too often, are guilty of focusing on faults you perceive in yourself and the things you have done long ago. What is done is done and should be forgiven (released). There is nothing you can do to change it. Your punishment of yourself for past mistakes only keeps you in a prison. The only escape from that prison is forgiveness. An attitude of love and kindness towards yourself is your key to the doors that hold you bound and give pain. Letting the past go opens the future to a bright new possibility.

Treat others with love, forgiveness, and compassion. Prejudices and old wounds must be released for you to go forward in your life. Holding resentments against someone is like holding a sword above your own head. As you strike the other person, you only strike yourself. So often, others are acting out of pain in their own lives, so it's not a personal attack on you. It could have been against anyone handy at the moment. One of the greatest truths is that the problem with which you are faced is not the real problem—your reaction to the problem is the problem. Learn to react with love, forgiveness and compassion.

Know that the universe is on your side. God is the energy behind the universe and God does not attack. All of the events—tornadoes, hurricanes, earthquakes, divorces, deaths, etc.—are simply events. Fear is an attractive force for events such as these. God loves you and would never plan to hurt you. The things that happen give you opportunities for growth and forgiveness.

Take time to be still and listen to your inner voice. Just a little time each day to do your devotional work makes a world of difference to the remainder of the day.

Rise above your negative thinking and addictions. You only hurt yourself with these things. Life becomes a living hell on earth as you find yourself controlled by something or someone outside yourself such as food, drugs, or cigarettes. Giving your power away to addictions reduces your experience of Life Force, or energy, and weakens you considerably.

I will be still, and let the earth be still along with me. And in that stillness we will find the peace of God. It is within my heart, which witnesses to God Himself.

Workbook, pg. 391

I have said that you cannot change your mind by changing your behavior, but I have also said, and many times, that you can change your mind. When your mood tells you that you have chosen wrongly, and this is so whenever you are not joyous, then know this need not be.

Text, pg. 63

The Nature of God

*"All invention, art literature, government, law and wisdom that has
come to the race has been given to it through those who have
deeply penetrated the secrets of nature and the mind of God."*

- Dr. Ernest Holmes, *The Science of Mind*

God's center is everywhere and God's radius is infinite. To try
to define God is to limit Him to words, and God is so much
more than words could ever describe. At one point in time, God
desired to create the universe. One theory is that He filled it with
His children so that He could experience Himself from a different
perspective. He had only Himself to use as building materials. He
had only His Creative Thoughts as a power to use to mold Himself
into physical forms. Therefore the universe consists of only the
basic building blocks out of which all matter is formed. All matter
is composed of energy at different levels of activity; therefore you
might suppose that in one sense, God is energy. The physical
universe is nothing but God solidified into form. God desired to
create humankind in order to have a medium of expression. God
created the human form and then extended Himself to that form
and breathed the breath of life into it. The basic building blocks
are the same, only the form being different. You are an extension
of God. You are spirit in physical form. You are a divine
expression of God. The truth about you is that you are spirit. You
are the Christ principle, the crystal clear awareness, and your will
is one with the Will of God. The Mind of God is the Mind with
which you think.

You and your brothers, along with your ego, made the world
and all of its distortions with your perceptions of it. You perceived
of yourself as "little." This perception brought fear of the future
and regret for your past into your awareness. A friend of mine lost
a kidney at an early age. As a result, he was unable to participate
in as many activities as he would have liked to. He was very
angry, and he is angry still. He blames God for taking away his
kidney and his happiness. His health has been poor all of his life
as a result. This perception of "littleness" is an insult, a
blasphemy to the spirit that you are and the God that created
you. When you settle for less in life than you deserve, this is also

34

belittling the Spirit that created you. How many things in your life are you settling for less than you want? God saves every loving thought you have ever had for you. These thoughts are your creations. God is Spirit. There is only one Son of God; we are all from the same Source and are all of the same nature.

God does not have a personality. He *is* Love. He *is* Abundance. He *is* Peace. He *is* Joy. He does not love. He *is* the Love that is within you, the love you give to others, and the love you receive from others. He expresses His characteristics through you and your fellow men.

God is real. God is Truth, Abundance, Health, Happiness, Harmony, and Strength. God is not "out there" somewhere, sitting on a cloud with a long white beard, sending people to Heaven or Hell according to His whim or according to their "sins."

God simply is. You are of the same nature, created in His likeness. You don't have to do anything. You don't have to love— you *are* love, so just allow that love to flow. Just let it be. Experience love to the full extent to which you are capable right now and know that it is God expressing through you. A rose doesn't have to do anything to smell like a rose. It *is* a rose. Its perfume naturally smells like a rose and it doesn't have to change anything. Anytime you catch yourself struggling, just relax and **be**.

God does not change His mind about you, for He is not uncertain of Himself…When anything threatens your peace of mind, ask yourself, "Has God changed His mind about me?"

Text, pg. 181

Surrounding me is all the life that God created in His Love. It calls to me in every heartbeat and in every breath, in every action and in every thought. Peace fills my heart, and floods my body with the purpose of forgiveness. Now my mind is healed, and all I need to save the world is given me. Each heartbeat brings me peace; each breath infuses me with strength. I am a messenger of God, directed by His Voice, sustained by Him in love, and held forever quiet and at peace within His loving Arms. Each heartbeat calls His Name, and every one is answered by His Voice, assuring me I am at home in Him.

Workbook, pg. 429

I said before that you are the Will of God. His Will is not an idle wish, and your identification with His Will is not optional, since it is what you are. Sharing His Will with me is not really open to choice, though it may seem to be. The whole separation lies in this error.

Text, pg. 135

Unlovable? No!

*I always remember that I have everything I need to enjoy my here
and now, unless I am letting my consciousness be dominated
by demands and expectations based on the dead past
or the imagined future.*

- Ken Keyes, Jr.

Were you born unlovable? How many babies are unlovable? No—you were born innocent and free! Your nature and your body are the sums of your expectations and your reactions to experiences from your parents, siblings, kids at school, etc. The "sins" of the fathers and the grandfathers are indeed visited upon the children. As a child, you were like a sponge, soaking up the judgments, perceptions and beliefs of those around you, and it is time to free yourself from those. Recognize your true nature as a Child of God—innocent and free. You go around looking for someone or something such as a teacher, a lecturer, a book, a class, or some other kind of torch that will restore to you your innocence, health, peace of mind, joy, love and life. I am truly sorry, but you will never find anyone who can carry your torch but yourself. Looking outside of one's self is looking in the wrong direction, for you carry your own torch and only you can light it and begin to live again by dropping your history, the "story" that you have been telling yourself all of your life.

Others can point you in the direction of your torch, but only you can pick it up, light it, and bring healing, love, and peace. How do you do this? No one can do it for you—you must look deep inside, recognize the lies that you have been told and that you have been telling yourself—they have been keeping you in a prison with no bars. You are free *right now!* You are innocent *right now.* That is your nature and your inheritance from your creator. Claim it and BE it. Release all those things that no longer serve you—you don't need them anymore. When you change your thinking and your perceptions and your judgments, you are born again. Relax—you don't have to struggle and "try" to do this, just stay in the now moment as much of your day as possible, for in each now moment is a new beginning, a time in which the past is gone and forgotten and the future does not threaten you.

Only you can return the original love to your recognition by acknowledging who you truly are—each moment of each day. As you do this, you will find that "problems" either go away easily and quickly or happen less often and to a lesser extremity. You will find that you attract others who will support you in your new life. You will find that you do not attract others to push your buttons or knock the chip off your shoulder because you have removed the buttons and the chip. Stand in your strength, be power-filled, and you will be full-filled!

The journey to God is merely the awakening of the knowledge of where you are always, and what you are forever. It is a journey without distance to a goal that has never changed.

Text, pg. 150

Your worth is not established by teaching or learning. Your worth is established by God . . . Nothing you do or think or wish or make is necessary to establish your worth.

Text, pg. 54

To accept your littleness is arrogant, because it means that you believe your evaluation of yourself is truer than God's.

Text, pg. 179

The holiest of all the spots on earth is where an ancient hatred has become a present love.

Text, pg. 562

Relationships

*You don't develop courage by being happy in your relationships
everyday. You develop it by surviving difficult times and
challenging adversity.*

- Barbara De Angelis

There is a story about how Sir Gawain was told that he had a
year to find out what women wanted most or he would die. His
conclusion was that *he would have her be what she had to be.*
That was what the woman wanted most; to be allowed just to be
the way she had to be. This is what all desire.

Looking for love in a relationship is often one of the ways in
which you fail to find it—because it is found only in yourself.
Most are looking for love in all the wrong places, as the song says.
Are you constantly looking to another person for your safety,
security, strength, spirituality, love, happiness, joy, whatever?
What do you lack? Find it in her; find it in him; find it in them;
find it in the physical or the event. The ego urges you to seek for
happiness but not to find it. Your happiness could never be found
in another place, person, job, house, car, or any place outside of
yourself. No one else in this world is responsible for your
happiness except yourself. No thing is capable of giving you
happiness. Do whatever is necessary to make that connection and
make it real. It is easy to write these words down in this book, but
living them in this world can be difficult. There seems to be so
much going against you.

Both partners in a relationship must heal themselves before
entering into a relationship. Focus on working on yourself, loving
yourself, and appreciating yourself and you will be ready to
attract people from which to choose. Choosing the right person
may be a challenge. Be prepared to keep trying and to be open to
Holy Spirit's guidance through prayer and meditation until
success is reached. The Holy Relationship referred to in **A Course
in Miracles** is the joining of two who are not meeting their needs
through the other, but are aware that they must look to
themselves for that fulfillment. Their love cannot be contained in
their relationship, but must be shared with the whole world. The
Holy Relationship is one in which both parties are willing to deal

honestly with each other at all times, not needing to take anything from each other. A Holy Relationship is where two come together, not seeking to control or use each other.

The holy relationship . . . is the old, unholy relationship, transformed and seen anew. The holy relationship is a phenomenal teaching accomplishment. . . . Be comforted in this; the only difficult phase is the beginning. For here, the goal of the relationship is abruptly shifted to the exact opposite of what it was. This is the first result of offering the relationship to the Holy Spirit, to use for His purposes.

Text, pg. 362

Those who offer peace to everyone have found a home in Heaven the world cannot destroy.

Text, pg. 527

It is not up to you to change your brother, but merely to accept him as he is. . . . Any attempt you make to correct a brother means that you believe correction by you is possible and this can only be the arrogance of the ego.

Text, pgs. 167-168

Under His (Holy Spirit) teaching every relationship becomes a lesson in love.

Text, pg. 312

Relationships, Part B

Whenever you're in conflict with someone, there is one factor that can make the difference between damaging your relationship and deepening it. That factor is attitude.

- Timothy Bentley

The appearance of the body is not a bar to experiencing a successful relationship. Too often people believe that they can't attract another because of a physical characteristic they possess. However, the personality and character of a partner is more important than the physical in the long run. Once people get to know you, love transcends the physical. If you express warmth, love and kindness in your dealings with people, this is what truly attracts one person to another. Purely physical relationships do not usually last, or at least, are often not as fulfilling as are spiritual ones.

All relationships start out as "special" relationships, that is, relationships that are based on ego needs. If you are in a relationship, there is always something to be learned in it. *If you and your partner are in perfect agreement, one of you is unnecessary.*

A relationship has been described as a two diamonds that are kept polished and shining by the friction between them. In other words, when things get tough in a relationship that is when the relationship is getting good. You always have the option to rid yourself of the irritation, but if the lesson still has not been learned, you will attract another person to help you to learn that lesson.

When a partner in a relationship supports the other's addictions, for example, an alcoholic, then the spouse is helping them to stay stuck. This is called codependency. A short definition of a codependent person is one who, when dying, sees someone else's life pass before their eyes. This condition is one where a person depends on another for their strength, their opinions, their leadership, etc. This is a sick relationship, dependent upon neediness and lack. It may be that only one of the partners carries the mark of codependency. There is a wonderful 12 Step program available to help—Codependents

Anonymous (CODA).

Staying in an abusive relationship is not recommended. There are many types of abuse. All of them are cause for a parting of the ways. But, healing takes place more quickly while in a relationship. Otherwise, you usually find someone else who pushes your buttons in the same way and gives you another chance to heal.

Marriages are not necessarily meant to last the rest of the partner's lives. Marriages that last 50-60 years might have lasted that long out of comfort, habit, or fear. There often comes a time when partners grow in different directions, when there is a need for a parting of ways. "Until death do us part" means until the death of the relationship you stay together. There is often a tendency to stay in a relationship. Fear of change, financial dependency, or because of the children, are some of the reasons.

1) Fear of change—the old status quo—holds one in a very harsh and unforgiving prison;

2) Financial dependency—indicates a lack of self—esteem; and

3) The children would be better off in a peaceful home without both parents than in a home where the parents are continually fighting or constantly in emotional upheavals.

If both parties are willing to relinquish themselves and their relationship to the Holy Spirit they will experience a Holy Relationship. This love is not exclusive. It is shared with all. The physical form may be different, but love is of God. It is not a human quality. It is not to be given to one of God's children and kept from another. You can form a Holy Relationship with everyone you meet. Be forgiving and compassionate towards others who are sharing this world with you. They are giving you opportunities to practice love and forgiveness in many ways.

I have said repeatedly that the Holy Spirit would not deprive you of your special relationships, but would transform them. And all that is meant by that is that He will restore to them the function given them by God. The function you have given them is clearly not to make happy. But the holy relationship shares God's purpose, rather than aiming to make a substitute for it. Every special relationship you have made is a substitute for God's Will, and glorifies yours instead of His because of the illusion that they are different.

Text, pg. 358

…exempt no one from your love, or you will be hiding a dark place in your mind where the Holy Spirit is not welcome. And thus you will exempt yourself from His healing power; for by not offering total love you will not be healed completely.

Text, pg. 244

As God sent me to you so will I send you to others. And I will go to them with you, so we can teach them peace and union.

Text, pg. 144

The Power
And the Glory

He is the best sailor who can steer within fewest points of the wind, and exact a motive power out of the greatest obstacles.

- Henry David Thoreau

Yours is the power and the glory, forever; the power and the glory, forever. Amen. Yours is the choice, the power and the glory, complete victimhood, poverty and misery, or some gradient between. Where do you want your life to be? It's up to you. You have the power to rise above life's thorns and barbs to experience a new day. If you are just a little miserable, or very much so, the tendency is to dwell on your failures, and how things, people, and situations have failed you or you have failed them.

Where do you want to be right now? Consider that maybe you are in the right place right now! Maybe the issues you are facing, whether they are in your employment, your relationships, your health, or some other of the myriad issues that humankind faces, have been drawn to you by yourself. It is possible that you were in a flat place in your spiritual growth and needed the boost (ever been hit in the head by a cosmic 2x4 before?) that these issues bring up for you. You are aware, subconsciously, of your needs and take steps to provide events from outside yourself to provoke the development of your inner strength.

Just relax. Let go. Rise above and free yourself from bondage, pain, and turmoil. God doesn't see the turmoil and troubles of the world because they are not real; He did not create them. *Yours* is the glory. *You* are so much greater than you can even imagine that you are. *You* are a Child of God, in whom He is well pleased. Celebrate yourself. You need do nothing but see the world with new eyes, with real eyes, and realize that God loves you and wants the best for you.

Because your Creator creates only like Himself, you are like Him. You are part of Him Who is all power and glory, and are therefore as unlimited as He is.

Text, pg. 141

The mind that serves the Holy Spirit is unlimited forever; in all ways, beyond the laws of space and time unbound by any preconceptions, and with strength and power to do whatever it is asked.

Workbook, pg. 382

In the darkness you have obscured the glory God gave you, and the power He bestowed upon His guiltless Son. All this lies hidden in every darkened place, shrouded in guilt and in the dark denial of innocence. Behind the dark doors you have closed lies nothing, because nothing can obscure the gift of God. It is the closing of the doors that interferes with recognition of the power of God that shines in you. Banish not power from your mind, but let all that would hide your glory be brought to the judgment of the Holy Spirit, and there undone.

Text, pg. 289

You'll Never Walk Alone

"When you walk through a storm,
Hold your head up high,
And don't be afraid of the dark.
Walk on! Walk on!
With hope your heart,
And you'll never walk alone -
You'll never walk alone!"

- Richard Rodgers, Oscar Hammerstein – **Carousel**

There are many in this world who are lost in the dark. There are many who are alone and lost in the dark, and many who suffer grievous pain, shame, and guilt. Are you one of these? Do you wish for hope but can find none? Do you seek for the light, but are blind? You are never alone and lost—you could not be alone and lost, for God is right there, closer than hands and feet. He is in front, behind, above, below, and on each side of you, holding your hands. You can turn your back on Him, but He will not turn His Back on you. Let Him guide you. When things seem the darkest, He brings the light if you would but open your eyes. When chaos fills the air, He brings his peace and offers it to you. There is no hope—only certainty. There is no darkness—only light. There is no chaos—only peace and love. Open your heart and mind and soul to accept your heritage—to accept who and what you truly are—the perfect, whole, complete, and loved Child of God. Cherish yourself and cherish the Spirit of God that is your life. Claim it, own it, intend this love into your constant awareness, for where there is love, all else must follow.

Walk on through the wind
Walk on through the rain
And you'll never walk alone!
You'll never walk alone!

Spirit am I, a holy Son of God/ free of all limits, safe and healed and whole, free to forgive, and free to save the world.

Workbook, pg. 173

The great peace of the Kingdom shines in your mind forever but it must shine outward to make you aware of it.

Text, pg. 99

Together is your joint inheritance remembered and accepted by you both. 2 Alone it is denied to both of you. 3 Is it not clear that while you still insist on leading or on following, you think you walk alone, with no one by your side? 4 This is the road to nowhere, for the light cannot be given while you walk alone, and so you cannot see which way you go. 5 And thus there is confusion, and a sense of endless doubting as you stagger back and forward in the darkness and alone. 6 Yet these are but appearances of what the journey is, and how it must be made. 7 For next to you is One Who holds the light before you, so that every step is made in certainty and sureness of the road.

Text, pg. 651

Death and Dying

"Do not stand at my grave and weep,
I am not there, I do not sleep.
I am in a thousand winds that blow,
I am the softly falling snow.

I am the gentle showers of rain,
I am the fields of ripening grain.
I am in the morning hush,
I am in the graceful rush

Of beautiful birds in circling flight,
I am the starshine of the night.
I am in the flowers that bloom,
I am in a quiet room,

I am the birds that sing,
I am in each lovely thing.
Do not stand at my grave and cry,
I am not there. I do not die."

- Mary Frye

"My body shall pass but my work shall go on. And my spirit shall live on. Even when I am taken away I shall work with you all for the deliverance of the world with the message of God. Prepare yourselves for the glory of God. Charge yourselves with the flame of Spirit. . . . Falter no more, you who have heard these words. Follow the truth that God has sent . . . and you shall be forever blessed. God is ever calling you through the flute of my heart. I urge you-forget Him not! Our bodies may perish, but let our souls forever blaze like eternal stars in the heart of God."

- Paramahansa Yogananda, *The Divine Romance*

Christ taught a most valuable lesson—death is not to be feared. Death is overcome. Death is but a transformation from one form to another, a change of identity. The more you resist and fear it, the more painful the experience of death will be. Resistance often comes in the form of attachment. If you are strongly attached and have many attachments, you will probably find yourself in fear around the subject.

The process of dying is a natural one, however it happens. Many have expounded upon what happens after death—none of whom know from experience. Those who have had near-death experiences give a sense of what it may be like, but no one knows for sure. Christ said that in the Father's house is many mansions, but no clarification was given beyond that. Many believe in resurrection into another life form to continue lessons on this earth plane that were not completed during the previous lifetime. Many believe in hell and other levels of punishment for "sins" while on earth. I categorically deny that a loving God would send his children to an everlasting flame. God loves his children and wants them to be happy. Life is eternal because God created it. It cannot end. I simply do not know—I will wait to find out.

Living is joy, but death can only weep. You see in death escape from what you made. But this you do not see; that you made death, and it is but illusion of an end. Death cannot be escape, because it is not life in which the problem lies. Life has no opposite, for it is God. Life and death seem to be opposites because you have decided death ends life.

Manual for Teachers, ppg. 51-52

...nothing is accomplished through death, because death is nothing. Everything is accomplished through life, and life is of the mind and in the mind. The body neither lives nor dies, because it cannot contain you who are life.

Text, pg. 104

Problems

"The mark of ignorance is the depth of your belief in injustice and tragedy... What the caterpillar calls the end of the world, a Master calls a butterfly."

- Richard Bach, *Illusions*

A problem is a matter of perspective. Think of problems as challenges, rather than problems; if there were no problems, there would be no opportunities. A caterpillar struggling to escape from its dark cocoon into butterflydom *seems* to have a problem. He works and works to make it out, looking to the entire world like a victim. He can fly, but that cocoon has got to go! However, if you try to help him in his struggles, he will die, for those struggles force fluids into his wings and enable him eventually to fly. Circumventing the process doesn't help; it hurts.

Similarly with you. Your process, no matter what it appears to be, is your process. It may happen very fast, or it may take many reincarnations. Your cocoon consists of your issues with health, relationships, jobs, abundance, etc. Silently applaud everyone you meet, including yourself, in their struggles, seeing their highest and best in those struggles. Know they are not victims, anymore than the caterpillar is a victim. Praying for the removal of your problems is not the answer, because you do not consciously know your Soul journey. The "problems" are serving you on the highest level and only you can rid yourself of your cocoon and truly fly. You are purified through these problems. The short story of all this is—you can't "save" anyone—they don't need "saving" anyway. They are perfect where they are.

Any problem is capable of being viewed from a multiplicity of angles. From one point, the problem may appear as a brick wall twenty feet high, which goes in both directions forever, a formidable barrier. Viewed from above, it is just a line with no height at all. Another view might reveal it as a wall with doors or it could be seen as a picket fence that is easily stepped over. Be willing to look at the world from another viewpoint—one that simplifies to the simple spiritual nature of all things. With God, all things are possible. You, with God, are in the majority! You are on the side of the Angels. Ask Holy Spirit for help to see the situation differently. This is the greatest tool you have to help you in your growth. You can't do it alone; ask for help. Be thankful for your "problems" for they are there to help you to grow; be grateful for people in your life who bring with them problems or seem to be themselves problems, for they are your greatest teachers. They are your brothers in God. They reflect the secrets that you have hidden from yourself.

Your only problem has been solved! Repeat this over and over to yourself today, with gratitude and conviction. You have recognized your only problem, opening the way for the Holy Spirit to give you God's answer. You have laid deception aside, and seen the light of truth. You have accepted salvation for yourself by bringing the problem to the answer. And you can recognize the answer, because the problem has been identified.

Workbook, pg. 143

Be certain that any answer to a problem the Holy Spirit solves will always be one in which no one loses.

Text, pg. 539

Small Still Voice

Sometimes I don't know where I'm going
And I don't like where I've been
I've just got to close my eyes and go within
Till I find that place of solitude, and get back in touch with live
And listen very softly, to that small still voice

Telling me "My child, you are doing just fine.
You just got little off track, and started changing your mind
You know all the right answers
And you know just what to do
So let go, and let God, and love will see you through"

Oh, I can get caught up in the details
And I know I'm just like you
Letting all of these people tell me what I should do
But there always comes a point where I stop dead in my tracks
And realize the answer means letting go of all the facts

And this small still voice says
"girl, you're doing just fine. You just got a little off track
and started changing your mind. You know all the right answers
and you know just what to do.
So let go and let God, and Love will see you through.

"A Small Still Voice," Mitzi MacDonald, ©1995

The still small Voice for God is not drowned out by all the ego's raucous screams and senseless ravings to those who want to hear It. Perception is a choice and not a fact. But on this choice depends far more than you may realize as yet. For on the voice you choose to hear, and on the sights you choose to see, depends entirely your whole belief in what you are.

Text, pg. 456

The truth about you is so lofty that nothing unworthy of God is worthy of you.

Text, pg. 177

Is this a little Voice, so small and still. It cannot rise above the senseless noise of sounds that have no meaning. God willed not His Son forget Him. And the power of His Will is in the Voice that speaks for Him.

Text, pg. 646

Vision

*"It is only with the Heart that one can see rightly.
What is essential is invisible to the eye."*
- Antoine de Saint-Exupéry, *The Little Prince*

Your vision is like a movie projector, projecting out through your being and shining onto a screen. If you don't like the movie, it doesn't do any good to change the screen; the film is the origin of the movie. What you see on your life screen has only one origin—your mind. You are the screenwriter, the director, the producer, the actor, and the gofer in the movie of your life. Actually, what you see with your physical eyes is only your judgment. Nothing else. It only seems real. Your judgment system doesn't allow you to see the real object (person, place, thing, event); the truth of that is spiritual. You see no thing as it really is—a person or a chair—with your physical eyes, as the world is nothing but a framework for your decisions about how things must be or a confirmation of how others have told you things must be.

What you wish to hide in yourself, you perceive in someone else and tend to criticize him or her bitterly for it. Your judgments and issues are showing up and those people are the screens that reflect them back to you. Children are perfect screens of your consciousness showing up in form. Even your pet's behavior is a reflection of your thinking. These are hard lessons to take sometimes, but they are, nevertheless, true. Your ego is very skillful at deluding you. When you "see" murder or war or hate or sin, some part of you has that consciousness.

Your vision actually improves when you close your physical eyes—what you see with them only tends to confuse. Sometimes I think that a blind person is more blessed than the sighted person because they do not have the distractions of the physical. True vision is pure and untainted by thoughts of this world. They see to the heart of the matter, judging not. Lift your eyes unto the Heavens and clarify your perceptions. God is there in everything you see.

Christ's eyes are open, and He will look upon whatever you see with love if you accept His vision as yours. The Holy Spirit keeps the vision of Christ for every Son of God who sleeps. In His sight the Son of God is perfect, and He longs to share His vision with you.

Text, pg. 228

Think but an instant just on this; you can behold the holiness God gave His Son. And never need you think that there is something else for you to see.

Text, pg. 444

If nothing but the truth exists, right-minded seeing cannot see anything but perfection.

Text, pg. 39

What you see reflects your thinking. And your thinking but reflects your choice of what you want to see.

Workbook, pg. 237

Peace

*Dedicate yourself to the good you deserve and desire for yourself.
Give yourself peace of mind. You deserve to be happy.
You deserve delight.*

- Mark Victor Hansen

You can see peace in this insane world if you choose to do so. When the world is falling apart, it is easy to fall apart yourself if you aren't centered every moment in your power and truth. You have the choice to be at the eye of the hurricane, with chaos all around you. Inner peace is experienced in that moment of separation between the occurrence of an event and your reaction to it. As you spend more time in the moment you become able to recognize the reaction sooner, rather than reacting automatically. As you extend that moment, you spend more of your time at peace.

You are responsible for your perception of your world; you make the decision to see peace or chaos. You cannot blame God, the world, or the ego. Don't blame yourself, either, for you simply made a mistake. Everything that you experience you have, by definition, included in your world. What you don't experience, you have excluded. In other words, by your invitation and with your permission, *stuff* happens! Not by your *conscious* invitation, necessarily! You have the power to be in the right place at the right time for some incident to occur, whether you judge it as "good" or "bad." You have the power to bring people into your life to either bring you joy or sadness. Remember that "good" vs. "bad," and joy vs. sadness, are merely judgments. Wait for the blessing in every situation. It is always there. *Guilt is not recommended.*

Think of life as an eternal springtime, forever blossoming anew through your self-expression, in which you never grow old. Sometimes it rains on your parade. The difference between a happy life and a miserable one is how you think about it, your state of mind. You could be miserable living in Hawaii if that is your choice. There are probably quite a few people there who fall into that category. You could choose to be at peace in a concentration camp. It has been done. It's your choice! Decide for peace instead of hatred, anger and war. The smallest pain you send to your brother becomes a dagger to yourself. No one can disturb your peace but you because it is God's Peace within you— the peace that passeth human understanding. *Go to peace instead of to pieces!*

Peace is impossible to those who look on war. Peace is inevitable to those who offer peace. How easily, then, is your judgment of the world escaped! It is not the world that makes peace seem impossible. It is the world you see that is impossible. Yet has God's Judgment on this distorted world redeemed it and made it fit to welcome peace. And peace descends on it in joyous answer.

Manual for Teachers, pg. 29-30

You have the right to all the universe; to perfect peace, complete deliverance from all effects of sin, and to the life eternal, joyous and complete in every way, as God appointed for His Holy Son.

Text, pg. 538

Can you imagine what it means to have no cares, no worries, no anxieties, but merely to be perfectly calm and quiet all the time.

Text, pg. 301

Holy child of God, when will you learn that only holiness can content you and give you peace?

Text, pg. 308

Searching

It is the experience of living that is important, not searching for meaning. We bring meaning by how we love the world..

- Bernie S. Siegel

All are searching for God. Many are searching in all the wrong places—in work, in money, in sex, in drugs, in play, in art, in cars, in sports, in thrills, in relationships, etc. There are thousands of ways to lose way, but the most basic, underlying, driving need of humankind is for the presence of God in their lives. The thirst and starvation of the spirit stems from the ignorance of the individual of his relationship to God. Humankind has developed an imagined "hole" in the psyche that drives it to the bottoms of the oceans and the ends of the universe, seeking but not finding that which is truly fulfilling. The thirst and starvation are not physical, but they are just as life threatening.

The busy-ness of life these days sends you scurry-ing and hurry-ing, do-ing and get-ting, to-ing and fro-ing. You are a human *be*-ing, not a human *do*-ing. You search everywhere for something to fill that hole—something to make you "whole." What you don't realize while all this is happening is that you are a *spiritual* being. You are having a physical experience, but the truth is that your basic nature is spiritual. You are searching in the physical world for a spiritual experience and no matter where you search in that realm; you are looking in the wrong direction. For ages now, the search has been misdirected, with humankind torn in half, going in circles, chasing its' tail. The direction that is correct is inward. *Within you* is the light. *Within you* is the truth. The search begins and ends there. Lemon juice is not obtained by squeezing an orange because there is no lemon juice *in* an orange. Pretending that you are not spiritual is like hiding your lamp under a bushel.

The source of your strength lies not in someone else or somewhere else. It does not come through money or physical power of any kind. Strength comes from your innermost core—the center of your being. One doesn't look for the strength of a tree in its' branches, but in its' roots and trunk. One doesn't look to the source of the Sun in its' rays, nor the strength of the ocean in its' waves. No. The mighty wave on the beach without the power of the ocean behind it is just a puddle of water. In God is the only true strength. In God is the only true love. Seek not outside. Seek not in the shallows for depth, in the meaningless for meaning, or in the liar for truth. There *is* nothing outside of you! It is all an illusion because you look through colored lenses of perception and your perception depends upon your history or someone else's opinion.

Within this kingdom the ego rules, and cruelly. And to defend this little speck of dust it bids you fight against the universe. This fragment of your mind is such a tiny part of it that, could you but appreciate the whole, you would see instantly that it is like the smallest sunbeam to the sun, or like the faintest ripple on the surface of the ocean. In its amazing arrogance, this tiny sunbeam has decided it is the sun; this almost imperceptible ripple hails itself as the ocean. Think how alone and frightened is this little thought, this infinitesimal illusion, holding itself apart against the universe. The sun becomes the sunbeam's "enemy" that would devour it, and the ocean terrifies the little ripple and wants to swallow it. Yet neither sun nor ocean is even aware of all this strange and meaningless activity.

Text, pg. 391

Rest in His Love and protect our rest by loving.

Text, pg. 128

Casting of Pearls

For truth is precious and divine, too rich a pearl for carnal swine.

- Samuel Butler

The urge to "save" someone from their "sins," to change them, to redirect their course, to judge them as being "lost," to enlighten them to your way of thinking, is simply and purely casting pearls before swine. It doesn't pay to try to teach a pig to sing—you just waste your time and annoy the pig! Teaching through preaching and manipulating just does not work in the long run. Either a person is ready to hear or they are not. Either the person is at a point in their life where their mind is open to a new way of thinking or it is not. This is not to call people swine, or pigs, but is simply a metaphor for the person whose mind is closed. You can talk, preach, and sing to the person with the closed mind all day and all night long and the only result is that they become more stubborn and closed minded, developing more arguments. The bottom line in this is that in your teaching do not expect results. If you teach love through your attitudes and behaviors, you are planting seeds that will grow in the future, maybe years later.

The individual who has become somewhat enlightened tends to mourn for those who trod another path. Judge not, lest ye be judged. Judge not, for you do not have all the facts for another person. Only God can judge truly and His judgment is that His Children are one with Him—whole, perfect and complete in every way. Everyone is in his perfect place in a perfect universe. The person who goes to church other than yours is going to the place that serves him the best at this time of his life. The person who goes to no church is being served perfectly. The person who does drugs and "terrible" things is going through a time when they know not who and what they are. They have forgotten that they are Children of God and they have lost their way. They are not "bad. Their actions may be antisocial to the extreme, but they are still spiritual expressions of God who have gone astray.

Just relax and live your life as best you can, knowing that you are teaching love, and love will have its way.

As condemnation judges the Son of God as evil, so open-mindedness permits him to be judged by the Voice for God on His behalf. As the projection of guilt upon him would send him to hell, so open-mindedness lets Christ's image be extended to him. Only the open-minded can be at peace for they alone see reason for it.

Manual for Teachers, pg. 16

Only one equal gift can be offered to the equal Sons of God, and that is full appreciation.

Text, pg. 105

Of your ego you can do nothing to save yourself or others, but of your spirit you can do everything for the salvation of both.

Text, pgs. 55-56

Fear

Be strong and of a good courage, fear not, nor be afraid... for the
Lord thy God, he it is that doth go with thee; he will not fail thee,
nor forsake thee.

The world is not a safe place. If you are looking for safety, you will not find it here. You can go to great lengths to try to protect yourself, but if death is your Soul's choice, death will find you (actually, you will find death). The billionaire can spend his fortune to construct a "safe" place, an underground haven stocked with all he needs for sustenance of life—from people to food to entertainment, air, water, doctors and nurses, an operating room, etc., etc., etc, and still be unable to avoid death.

Fear is the great motivator. Fear of the unknown, fear of punishment from a God against whom he had "sinned," fear of a God to whom he had lied and had cheated, fear of a God who is seen as unreasonably angry, violent and vindictive. He cries out "Why me?" to a God who obviously doesn't really care. What else can he expect from such a God but punishment?

You are taught fear from the moment of conception. Fear is not a natural thing, however. It is carefully installed in the psyche. Your parents, teacher, and churches deliberately teach fear. I'm not saying that it is wrong to look both ways when crossing the street, for example, or being careful around strangers. Caution is not a bad thing. Rev. Kay Hunter in Carrollton, TX says that she locks the house and car, not from fear, but so as not to tempt people who might have the disposition to steal.

Fear is the great cancer of society, the great "Satan" of humankind. Fear of tomorrow, fear of the stranger at the door, fear of staying, fear of going. Fear builds your prison and fear keeps you in it. For some, dying is preferable to the prospect of the pain involved in breaking out of that prison. Somehow, that atmosphere of fear becomes a security blanket, a place with which you are at least familiar and that is preferable to the terrible unknown monster that lurks, waiting to pounce.

Do you expect the worst to happen? Fear has an attractive nature. If you are frightened of developing a cancer, or gaining weight, for example, the conditions are more likely to happen. The body is vulnerable to your thoughts. I know when I am working around the house and drop a screw or nail, the fear would hit me automatically that it should be hard to find. That has been my experience, and inevitably, that is what happens. As soon as I drop it, fear comes in and tells me that it is lost. You often fail to act because you are afraid and by your inaction invite that which you most feared, thus setting yourself up for failure. By acting out of fearful thinking, you often bring about reactions from others and this accomplishes that which you were trying to avoid. It sometimes seems that you are damned before you begin, that there is no way out. There operates, in this world, the Law of Cause and Effect (Karma) what goes around comes around. People and events and even things seem to conspire to fulfill your most fearful thoughts. Thoughts are powerful things that are seeds planted in a fertile mind, to grow either immediately or sometime later. Karma doesn't really exist, though; it is an illusion. However, if you believe in it, it is real.

Fear is attractive for many. Witness the popularity of bungee jumping, parachuting, racing, roller coasters, etc. The ego has quite a time with fear as the greatest tool in its arsenal. What *A Course in Miracles* calls your "split mind" constantly spins from love to fear, from highs to lows, from light to darkness, in a chaotic dance. You search outside of yourself for salvation when there is actually nothing outside yourself—the world is but a framework upon which you hang your thoughts, perceptions, and expectations. You become a slave to the forces of darkness and gather witnesses to agree you as to how terrible things are and how someone else is to blame. These forces of darkness extend "man's inhumanity to man" mentality around the globe.

Underlying all this is the fact that this world is all an illusion, a lie. There actually is *nothing* to fear. At one time I was in a public park. It was twilight, and it was kind of scary. I needed to use the restroom and went in just as someone was coming out. The light was on, but after I sat down the light went off. My mind filled with fear of being attacked. I spent some time listening for someone, but no sounds came. Finally, I got up and went out of the cubicle, fumbled my way to the door, only to find out that the light was on a timer and had gone out automatically.

Love is the answer! God is on the job! The universe works for your highest and greatest good. The activity of your consciousness forms your Soul's journey. As you forgive others and release fearful thoughts, you attract love into your life, rather than chaos. Do not join in the perspective of this "veil of tears". Heal your "split mind" as you look to Holy Spirit for relief from fear and to replace it with joy. Rise above the illusory world to see the beauty that God sees. Walk through the valley of the shadow of death, fearing no evil because God did not create evil—evil is only living backwards. There is no sin—only the errors that you commit out of ego thinking. God's final judgment is that you are His Beloved Son, in whom He is well pleased.

Of course, you cannot hold this position every second of every day. You fall down, you slip, and you screw up. When this happens, forgive yourself for your errors, your ego-thoughts; let go of fear, guilt, and remorse, get up and start over, knowing God loves you and has already forgiven you.

The presence of fear is a sure sign that you are trusting in your own strength. The awareness that there is nothing to fear shows that somewhere in your mind, though not necessarily in a place you recognize as yet, you have remembered God, and let His strength take the place of your weakness. The instant you are willing to do this there is indeed nothing to fear.

Workbook, pg. 77

You can indeed afford to laugh at fear thoughts, remembering that God goes with you wherever you go.

Workbook, pg. 64

What is not love is always fear, and nothing else.

Text, pg. 325

Attack Thoughts
Towards Self

*Be gentle with yourself, learn to love yourself, to forgive yourself,
for only as we have the right attitude toward ourselves can we
have the right attitude toward others.*

- Wilfred Peterson

The harmful attack thoughts you have for yourself poison your
life with bitterness. You are often your own worst critic, much
harder on yourself than on your worst enemy. If someone else
spoke to you or a friend as you do to yourself, you would be
violently angry with that person! Every moment of every day is an
opportunity to give yourself a break—to forgive yourself for
mistakes you have made, mistakes you are making, and mistakes
you are about to make. Spend some time every day being aware of
your thoughts towards yourself. How do you feel when you look in
the mirror? Do you even look in the mirror? When you make a
mistake, what is the message that you hear in your mind? When
someone appears to be avoiding you, what is your assumption?
What have you learned from your parents as to how to think
about yourself? What have your siblings and fellow students
taught you? How about your fellow workers? This is a call for
forgiveness—letting go of all attack thoughts. As soon as one
enters your mind, say to yourself, "Cancel!" or "Delete!"

*...attack thoughts must entail the belief that you are vulnerable, their effect
is to weaken you in your own eyes. Thus they have attacked your perception
of yourself. And because you believe in them, you can no longer believe in
yourself. A false image of yourself has come to take the place of
what you are.*

Workbook, pg. 41

The Bottom Line

Change your thoughts and you change your world..

- Norman Vincent Peale

Let's cut to the bottom line, here. Have you gone to classes, read books, prayed, attended lectures, gone to church, and meditated for years? Where has that gotten you? Do you still have problems—problems with disease, finances, relationships, weight, and jobs—all or some of the above? It is time to stop playing small, being the victim, sick, or in pain. You are *not* small. You are only as small as you think you are. You are *not* victims of anything but your own thinking. Any sickness or pain that you experience is of your own construction. You are all committing suicide little by little. You are the scriptwriter of your life, the captain of your Soul, the master of your life.

Any time you think you are anything less than perfect, whole, and complete, you are belittling the One Who created you. When you look for your truth outside of yourself, you are telling the world that the knowledge of truth that God gave you as your heritage has been forgotten. If you don't know what to do, you are lying to yourself. You know. Recognize that you have the answers. You have *all* the answers and you have had them all the time. Now the question becomes: "How?" How do you change your life? How do you change your thinking? How do you change the person(s) with whom you are in relationship? How do you get control of your inner child's wants, wants, and wants? How do you resist that piece of cake or serving of potatoes and gravy? How do you start exercising when you so hate to do it? How do you get a job? How you get a better job? How do you get enough money to live comfortably? How do you find that perfect prince or princess amongst all these turkeys? Why is it happening to you *again*?

All of the excuses that you have had and the blame you have put on others only distracts you from your innermost goal. You might even have lots of proof and other people to witness to the fact that the world has done you wrong. Your innermost goal, although hidden deep within you, is to experience a greater oneness with God. You can't experience that oneness in the past or in the future. You can't experience it when you are blaming others or yourself. You can't experience it when you think of yourself as weak, even though others might have told you that you were weak—it isn't true.

You *are* capable of prayer without ceasing—carrying God in your hearts at all times and in all situations. You are capable of constantly being *in* the world, but not *of* it, also. You are also capable of being in the NOW times of your life, day after day, minute after minute, and second after second. That is the key. Going unconscious into worry over what happened in the past or what might happen in the future only distracts you from the most precious moment in your lives—the moment of NOW. Worry never solved any problem. If it won't be a problem 10,000 years from now, don't take it so seriously. You *already* have the answers, and searching outside of yourself only leads to frustration and failure.

There are some who seem to be so lost that they are not motivated to change their lives. Those will find their way eventually. Sometimes they have to "bottom out" to achieve enough pain to get their attention and get motivated. Then they can discover that there is a better way of thinking, a better way of living than the one they are experiencing. Bless them in their growth.

The basic and overriding question of your life is: *How do you change your thinking?* You only are capable of thinking one thought at a time—that is a physical fact. You are present at the time that you are thinking that one thought—another physical fact. Now, whether you are *really* present or not is another question! Your busyness is the thing that gets you into trouble. You tend to get caught up in the distractions of the world, the goings and comings, the chaos and tragedies. The ego uses anything and everything to distract you from your true goal. The answer to changing your thoughts is to keep returning, moment-by-moment, to your Source and not reacting to what you see in the world, to *create* rather than *react.* "Stuff" happens. Don't go up on a mountaintop to get away from the world! Rise above the world from within the world! Observe from a distance. Separate yourself from events in the world.

Just do it! Do it now—don't put it off any longer, whatever it is! Take steps in the direction that you want to go. Stop whining and complaining. Stop being a victim; stop looking outside yourself for healing of any sort. Stop acting the game of being small, out of control, and weak. You are power-filled and capable of overcoming worldly conditions. Look to your Source for fulfillment. Change is the common denominator of the universe—look forward to it, rather than resisting!

And for each witness to the body's death He sends a witness to your life in Him Who knows no death. Each miracle He brings is witness that the body is not real. Its pains and pleasures does He heal alike, for all sin's witnesses do His replace.

Text, pg. 580

A sense of separation from God is the only lack you really need correct.

Text, pg. 14

Anger always involves projection of separation, which must ultimately be accepted as one's own responsibility, rather than being blamed on others.

Text, pg. 91

The Bottom Line, Part B

The bottom line is that (a) people are never perfect, but love can be,
(b) that is the one and only way that the mediocre and vile can be
transformed, and (c) doing that makes it that. We waste time
looking for the perfect lover, instead of creating the perfect love.

- Tim Robbins

If finances are a challenge, realize at the very deepest level that God's Abundance is yours right now and the knowledge that God has given you will help you to find the ways to overcome this challenge. Most people who are having financial problems are stepping on their own supply line, not feeling they are good enough to receive that ready abundance. Also, giving is the key to receiving—it opens up that pipeline.

If weight is a challenge, the only food you *really* need is from God. Diets don't really work in the long run and you *can* control of your consumption. That donut doesn't control you; you are bigger than it. Releasing weight becomes easy when you truly desire to do so. Exercising becomes easy when you truly desire to release weight and help your body to become a fit temple of God.

Finding a job becomes easy when you claim your strength and wisdom given you by God. Very few people can resist hiring one who is filled with true love and power. If you are dissatisfied with the job you now have, forgive it, forgive yourself, and throw yourself into the job completely. When you are ready and have learned the lessons required at that place, a new job will show up. If you are looking for a job, know that the perfect job is looking for you, *right now!* Relax. Don't get caught up in worry and thoughts of lack. There are many jobs out there! When you are ready, truly ready, it will show up.

Relationships are a challenge for many. You can't force your partner into a mold that he/she doesn't fit! You can't change anyone but yourself! Relationships are places in which you learn about yourself, so stop blaming your partner and take responsibility for healing the relationship. If this relationship is not right for you, another will appear after you have done your work in your current relationship. Finding a life partner becomes an exercise in finding yourself, loving yourself, forgiving any earlier relationships, and forgiving yourself. When all that is accomplished, the road becomes open for a partner to join your path.

If health is a challenge, know that the mind-body connection is very real. What goes on in the body starts first in the mind. All conditions are *fluid* and can change, no matter how "serious" the situation may appear to be. Be open to those changes. Don't resist or resent the situation. Utilize doctors and other healing modalities, as necessary. Be happy in the place where you are, when your thoughts are at peace. This opens up a space where healing can take place. Love yourself and know that you are healing right now. Love yourself exactly the way you are. Be open to living a useful and productive life, no matter what physical limitations you may have.

If your children have become a challenge, God bless you. Children are *meant* to be challenges. Children stress the limits of adult patience *because* they are children. That is the way it is. Love them anyway. They are learning. Provide a good role model for them; whether you think they are watching or not, they are picking up on your thoughts and inner feelings. They pick up on the smallest things that you think they don't notice. Talk to them and spend time with them, not lecturing, but learning from them how they feel and what they are thinking.

The abundance of Christ is the natural result of choosing to follow him.

Text, pg. 13

The law of creation is that you love your creations as yourself, because they are part of you.

Text, pg. 182

Forgive

God pardons like a mother, who kisses the offense into everlasting forgiveness.

- Henry Ward Beecher

The tool that the Holy Spirit has given us in this world is forgiveness. Forgive yourself and others—in your past and in your present. Forgive yourself and others for all things that were never done in this false universe that you have built. It is an illusion. It is *not* real! When it comes up and bites you on the behind, forgive. When you are dwelling on the past where it seems that you were "done wrong," forgive. Let it go. It does not serve you. Your guilt and your obsession with the things of this world keep you locked in and keep your brothers and sisters also locked in. Release yourself and humankind through your forgiveness. Often it is not enough to forgive just once, but as Christ taught, sometimes seventy times.

Together with forgiveness, it is important to be faithful to a spiritual practice. A spiritual practice is something you do on a daily basis to stay connected. Things like meditating, going to classes, going to church, reading spiritual books are all examples of practice. You can find all kinds of excuses to forget or to lapse in practice, so you must actively remember what the eventual results will be when that happens—the pain that fear and guilt bring. The Course urges you to be proactive and diligent, to be on the alert for any blocks that the ego brings to you to keep you from doing your spiritual practice.

The grace of God rests gently on forgiving eyes, and everything they look on speaks of Him to the beholder. He can see no evil, nothing in the world to fear, and no one who is different from himself.

Text, pg. 529

Shifting Your Perception

"If the doors of perception were cleansed,
everything would appear to man as it is, infinite."

-William Blake

A miracle, as defined in the Course, is a shift in perception. Christ talked about this in the Bible when he told you to turn the other cheek, to look at things from a different point of view, to see beyond the physical to the spiritual. I have been doing a lot of bicycle riding lately and it came to me that in biking, when you come to a hill and have to pedal harder, you shift into another gear. This makes the going easier.

What could you do if you hadn't been told that you couldn't do it? Jesus said that greater things than he did you can do. You have the innate power to "be all that you can be. You are already it. Live from that power consciously, day by day; take that step that is so "fearful" and know that there is no step that is "wrong." You can only fall into the Arms of God; there is nowhere else to fall. In life, when you find yourself in any sort of pain, financial, physical, relationship, job, whatever, all you need do is to rise above the so-called battleground and see the situation as something to be forgiven and released; shift into love. This world is insane and to try to make sense of it only makes the insanity more insane. Love is the answer. Love and forgiveness are the great healers in all areas of life.

It is essential it be kept in mind that all perception still is upside down until its purpose has been understood. Perception ... is the outward picture of a wish; an image that you wanted to be true.

Text, pg. 516

Polish Your Diamond

As you begin to understand the immense power and love you hold inside, you will find an unending surge of joy, light and love that will nourish and support you all the days of your life.

- Susan Jeffers

How bright is your diamond? How many facets does your diamond contain and how smooth are they? You might think it is strange that I ask these questions, but picture your life as a raw diamond from the ground, raw and rough. Look back on your life—the rough times, the rough places, the tough situations that you went through were the buffers that ground your stone smoother and smoother until became smooth and faceted, shining bright and beautiful in the light of the sun. So give thanks for those tough times and the tears and fears that went along with them as you look in the mirror. Give thanks for those times to come that will polish your diamond even more until you reflect God's Light and Love even more perfectly.

Every response you make is determined by what you think you are, and what you want to be is what you think you are. What you want to be, then, must determine every response you make.

Text, pg. 127

Your holy mind establishes everything that happens to you. Every response you make to everything you perceive is up to you, because your mind determines your perception of it.

Text, pg. 181

Seek Not
Outside Yourself

*If you want to take your mission in life to the next level, if you're
stuck and you don't know how to rise, don't look outside yourself.
Look inside. Don't let your fears keep you mired in the crowd.
Abolish your fears and raise your commitment level to the point of
no return, and I guarantee you that the Champion Within will burst
forth to propel you toward victory.*

- Bruce Jenner

I have hinted a few times in these articles that **you** are the
Source and now I am *telling* you that **you** are your **source**. Seek
not outside yourself, as the Course says. "Seek not outside
yourself for a guide." There is a new energy, these are new times,
and it is time to take responsibility for your own actions and your
own guidance. Throw away the old energy teachings and the old
energy books. Take responsibility for drawing that which you
need to your front door, and that which comes to your front door
will be appropriate to your level of consciousness. You who are
awakening to your true nature, changing your planet, are
bringing in the new energy. It is changing old tendencies and
prophecies. You are the teacher for those to come, and those who
don't want to participate will leave the planet. Surely these will be
chaotic times, for the resistance to these changes will be strong
and from all directions. There may be more wars and struggles;
look behind them to the eventual and positive outcomes. Love is
the answer to all things. Say "**yes**" to the new energy, to opening
up to being responsible, to being a teacher. Say "**yes**" to Spirit as
you glorify in the Love of Christ from within you. *(This message
was inspired from the messages from the entity Tobias. Read and
hear his messages at* http://www.crimsoncircle.com*)*

Be not afraid of love. For it alone can heal all sorrow, wipe away all tears, and gently awaken from his dream of pain the Son whom God acknowledges as His...Salvation asks you give it welcome. And this world awaits your glad acceptance, which will set it free.

Workbook, pg. 455

Healing and Enlightenment

The only work that will ultimately bring any good to any of us is the work of contributing to the healing of the world..

- Marianne Willamson

I want to talk today about healing. Healing is simply the process of becoming enlightened—of becoming more aware of the Light of Christ within you and around you. Healing happens when you notice how the old ways of fear and pain, things that used to work for you, simply do not serve you anymore. Healing happens when you make a decision to be happy rather than to be right, to be at peace, rather than going to pieces. The process of healing involves a side effect—the ego revolts against it. The more peaceful you become, the more the ego throws at you to disturb your peace. The ego, however, is but a part of your mind that wishes to divide you from God; its only power comes from your agreement with it. When you withdraw agreement, it whimpers away into a corner!

The practical side of healing is the release of negative energy that was stored in your mind and body during times of chaos. That energy gets released, and as it is released, it feels like chaotic symptoms are happening all over again; it certainly doesn't feel like healing!. You have to be patient as you heal and allow this release of energy rather than giving up and going back to the old ways. It might take a while to realize that your life has changed in certain ways and to take encouragement from that; journaling helps to record your feelings during this process, for you can read back in the journal and see how your life has been healed. Support from groups like twelve step programs, Course in Miracles study groups, or a Mastermind Group is very valuable also.

Healing is what we are here for; enjoy your fear, pain, and chaos as long as you choose. Just remember that the peace and love of God is always there for you and that Christ and the Holy Spirit are always there to hold your hand during the healing process.

Healing is accomplished the instant the sufferer no longer sees any value in pain.

Manual for Teachers, pg. 17

Our emphasis is now on healing. The miracle is the means, the Atonement is the principle, and healing is the result. To speak of "a miracle of healing" is to combine two orders of reality inappropriately. Healing is not a miracle. The Atonement, or the final miracle, is a remedy and any type of healing is a result. The kind of error to which Atonement is applied is irrelevant. All healing is essentially the release from fear. To undertake this you cannot be fearful yourself. You do not understand healing because of your own fear.

Text, pg. 23

Why wait for Heaven? Those who seek the light are merely covering their eyes. The light is in them now. Enlightenment is but a recognition, not a change at all...The light came with you from your native home, and stayed with you because it is your own...It shines in you because it lights your home, and leads you back to where it came from...

Workbook, pg. 357

It's an Inside Job

There is a fountain of youth: it is your mind, your talents, the creativity you bring to your life and the lives of the people you love. When you learn to tap into this source, you will truly have defeated age.

- Sophia Loren

You *are the Source of your abundance.* The abundance may physically originate from others, but it is created by you, through your consciousness. You provide the magnetic power that draws the abundance from known and unknown points of origin. If you seem to be surrounded by sharks in the form of debtors, remember that debtors cannot eat you. There are many ways of obtaining financial rearrangements. The debtors don't want to force you into a position where they won't get their money, so be nice to them and tell them your circumstances. Tell them how much you can pay and when; then follow through.

You are the Source of your health. The body is your vehicle on this plane of existence. There are a certain number of DNA factors involved. The way the body is treated (or in many cases, mal-treated) is another factor. Actually, putting too much emphasis on the body is a focus on duality. Your body is perfect, just the way it is. If you are sick, align yourself with spirit, see a physician or take medicine if it is called for, see a spiritual practitioner or a holistic practitioner, but know that you are the source of your health. Ultimately, you can heal yourself. There is no disease that has not had a "miracle" healing.

You are the Source of your circumstances. When things seem to be out of control, look again. What were the ways that you helped to make the situation possible? How does this situation serve you (what are the pay-offs)? You draw to you people and situations like a magnet. You have a built-in energy projector that says, "I have buttons that need to be pushed." Someone will come to you who has the energy level that needs to push buttons (yours in particular) and does just exactly that. Another thing, there is no such thing as an accident. Somewhere along the line the energetic forces of the universe brought people and the necessary timing together to create an "accident" that serves all parties.

There is a blessing behind the "accident." You may not see it for a long time, or never. Just know that it is there. This is a perfect universe you live in. Know that you are blessed in all circumstances.

You are the Source of your employment. Jobs seem to be a continuing challenge. If you are not currently employed, your perfect position is looking for you. The more distressed you become, the harder it will be for you to recognize that perfect job, even if it were sitting on your lap. Relax (see the above section on abundance). You might have to take two or three jobs while you are waiting for your job to show up. If you don't like it, simply align yourself with spirit and start looking for another position. Know that your perfect position is looking for you—where one door is closed, another one opens. Again, avoid stress and relax into the process.

You are the Source of your relationships. Relationships are the biggest learning experiences you can experience. You attract the persons who can teach you patience, or love, or trust, or whatever. The lessons can be painful if you resist them. I certainly don't recommend staying in an abusive situation, so if that is the case, get out immediately. I recommend staying in a relationship until your introspection tells you that you have learned the lessons that your partner is there to provide. You will know when that time comes; if you leave too early, the lessons are still there to be taught and the universe will simply provide another person who is similar to the one you left.

You are the Source of your addictions. All of us have addictions of one sort or another. The ego provides people, drugs, food, cigarettes, coffee, etc., to fulfill your need to separate yourself from God, as all of these things (and others) are simply ways to distract our attention from Spirit. Align with Spirit—take time to be still and listen to Spirit—to hear the sweet Voice of God from within you. Know that you are **not** a victim of the world or anything in it. You are a Creator. You are a Master. All that stuff you see out there is not real. Only Spirit—God—is real.

Love is always the answer.

Love is always the answer.

Love is always the answer,

and you are Love.

You are a Child of God, a priceless part of His Kingdom, which He created as part of Him. Nothing else exists and only this is real. You have chosen a sleep in which you have had bad dreams, but the sleep is not real and God calls you to awake.

Text, pg. 101

...understand what "The Kingdom of Heaven is within you" really means...the word "within" is unnecessary.
The Kingdom of Heaven is you.

Text, pg. 60

...nothing outside yourself can save you; nothing outside yourself can give you peace.

Workbook, pg. 119

The Land of Shadows:
Good and Evil

*"We do not see because we have eyes but because we see, we
have eyes. The eyes do not really see very much. Spiritual
discernment, which can be done by a blind person,
is not really seeing."*

- Helen Keller

This physical plane in which you live is nothing but a land of
shadows. It is but an illusion, obfuscating spiritual vision. It
confuses the issue, distracts the mind from spiritual principles.
There is value on this plane of existence because you came here
for a purpose—to grow spiritually—but it is very easy to use
things of this world to take the place of God in your life. See
beyond the shadow, beyond the physical, and beyond the
frustrations and activities of your daily life. It is important to
realize that things that seem important like earning a living,
raising a family, or getting an education are really only things to
occupy us while the real activity is going on. This activity is your
awakening to God, healing the apparent separation between God
and you. Humankind experiences many levels of pain here. All of
it is a stimulus to becoming more aware of who and what you are.
You are not small or helpless or weak.

On this physical plane you see much happening that either
feels good or doesn't and you have the tendency to call the first a
"good" thing, and the second, a "bad" thing. It is ok to discern one
thing from another—like light from dark, or red from blue—if you
don't judge the light and red as good and the dark and blue as
bad. The old story about the farmer whose son found a horse and
brought it home is very illustrative of this. The farmer's neighbor
exclaimed, "Oh, that's good!" And the farmer said, "We'll see." The
horse jumped the fence and ran away, and the farmer's neighbor
exclaimed, "Oh, that's bad!" And the farmer said, "We'll see." Then
the horse came back with a bunch of mares following behind,
farmer's neighbor exclaimed, "Oh, that's good!" And the farmer
said, "We'll see." Then while the farmer's son was breaking one of
the horses, he fell and broke his leg, and the farmer's neighbor

exclaimed, "Oh, that's bad!" And the farmer said, "We'll see." Then the army came through to take the older boys off to war, and the farmer's son couldn't go because of his leg, and farmer's neighbor exclaimed, "Oh, that's good!" And the farmer said, "We'll see." And so on. It may have not been just the farmer's neighbor that was exclaiming on the "goodness" and "badness" of these events—it might have been the whole village, the city, the state, the nation, or the world, that joined in agreement. It doesn't make any difference how many people agree, the judgments were not necessarily correct. You not only should not judge, you really *cannot* judge—you don't have all the facts.

Shadows are there because something is blocking the light. See the light. Focus on the light. Become one with the light.

Innocence is wisdom because it is unaware of evil, and evil does not exist. It is, however, perfectly aware of everything that is true. The resurrection demonstrated that nothing can destroy truth. Good can withstand any form of evil, as light abolishes forms of darkness.

Text, pg. 38

You must have noticed an outstanding characteristic of every end that the ego has accepted as its own. When you have achieved it, it has not satisfied you. That is why the ego is forced to shift ceaselessly from one goal to another; so that you will continue to hope it can yet offer you something.

Text, pg. 155

Victims

The word "victim" implies helplessness. Many victims believe there is a conspiracy in the world to attack them—to pull them down or to hurt their feelings. Are you a victim to circumstances outside of yourself? Are you able to control your reactions to events or people so that you can be happy regardless of them? Are your feelings out of control? Do they rage from high to low and back again? Feelings are important. I'm not putting feelings down, but they shouldn't be in control of your life.

You can become a victim to many things—your boss, your wife/husband, your children, your church, food, alcohol, cigarettes. The list goes on. Some people spend years in the Alcohol Anonymous program and end up ditching the alcohol habit while simultaneously gaining a dependence on cigarettes and/or AA itself. The problem is not in the person/substance to which you are a victim, but the missing ingredient in yourself, the lack in yourself that you are trying to fill.

You are whole, perfect, and complete, *right now*. You are not a victim—helpless. There is nothing missing. You are Spirit. Get off the cross; the world needs the timber!

You must have noticed an outstanding characteristic of every end that the ego has accepted as its own. When you have achieved it, it has not satisfied you. That is why the ego is forced to shift ceaselessly from one goal to another; so that you will continue to hope it can yet offer you something.

Text, pg. 155

Conscious Choices

*"You have made pathways in your brains through your thoughts.
As you go through your life—day by day—you build a pattern of
neuron attachments in your brain. Thus you become accustomed to
certain parts of your life that work and certain parts that don't
work. The idea here is that you have to look at the areas that aren't
working for you and open your mind to ways of thinking
that will not substantiate those pathways."*

- From the movie, "What the Bleep"

You see, energy, according to quantum physics, is simply a field of potentials. Look at your situation and search out alternate potentials of thinking and behaving that will negate your habitual neuron pathways. For example, many have concerns about weight. Look at your past behavior and ways that it can be changed, even in small ways. Then practice these over and over until your neuron attachments have been changed. Then find other ways of changing and practice these. Little by little, you will find your desires and actions conforming to one another. This is a very practical way of changing your thinking and changing your life. (*The Science of Mind*—Dr. Ernest Holmes) and making miracles by changing your perception (**A Course in Miracles**).

*Heaven is chosen consciously. The choice cannot be made until alternatives
are accurately seen and understood. All that is veiled in shadows must be
raised to understanding, to be judged again, this time with Heaven's help.
And all mistakes in judgment that the mind had made before are open to
correction, as the truth dismisses them as causeless. Now they are without
effects. They cannot be concealed, because their nothingness is recognized.*

Workbook, pg. 265

*If you knew Who walks with you on the way that you have chosen,
fear would be impossible.*

Text, pg. 378

*The Holy Spirit will help you reinterpret everything that you perceive
as fearful, and teach you that only what is loving is true.*

Text, pg. 81

Change

If one desires a change, one must be that change before that change can take place.

- Gita Bellin

Change is a great principle of life. You cannot depend on people, things, events, jobs, or most anything else to remain static. Change is the most constant thing there is—change happens. There are two aspects of change to discuss here.

First, people change. Circumstances change. People and pets die. People go away for one reason or another. People treat you badly. Jobs are eliminated. Sickness may come to your body. Change comes in many forms but what you are inside does not change. Don't let change destroy you—*don't take it personally*. Adjust to whatever change is going on out there. Be calm. Relax.

Second, making changes in your life. The only way to make real changes in your life is making a minute-by-minute, hour-by-hour recommitment to the change. For example, New Years resolutions don't usually work because there is no real commitment and follow up involved; there is no plan. Real change is not skin-deep. If it is important for you to change, no matter what the change involves, make a plan, follow through, recommit daily, evaluate your progress, and report to an impartial witness.

If you are honestly committed to evaluate your progress and forgive yourself for the times when you slip off the path, you have a great start. There will be times when someone else will try to lead you astray, for whatever reason. No one outside of yourself can control you unless you allow it to happen. Be firm and polite as you say, "No." "No" is a complete sentence; you don't have to give a reason if you don't wish to. Certainly you don't have to lie to save their feelings. Sometimes it might feel that, in trying to change, you are swimming upstream because your family and friends tend to resist change in you. It might change your relationship with them, or it might require a subsequent change in them. Simply decide to treat yourself kindly. Calmly and decisively decide to be kind to yourself and recommit each day. You are able to make the decision to be in charge and take the steps that you wish to improve.

Bear in mind that you don't need to change your basic nature. You are perfect, whole, and complete right now—and if you love yourself just the way you are, from that realization, you can simply make adjustments in your attitudes and behaviors so that they are in alignment with your basic nature. This alleviates the fear inherent in the word "change." Many would rather die than change, and often succeed in doing just exactly that.

Appearances deceive, but can be changed. Reality is changeless.
It does not deceive at all, and if you fail to see beyond appearances you are
deceived. For everything you see will change, and yet
you thought it real before, and now you think it real again.
Reality is thus reduced to form, and capable of change . . .
It is this that makes it real, and keeps it separate from all appearances.
It must transcend all form to be itself. It cannot change.

Text, pg. 642

. . . having learned that the changes in his life are always helpful, he must
now decide all things on the basis of whether they increase the helpfulness or
hamper it. He will find that many, if not most of the things he valued before
will merely hinder his ability to transfer what he has learned to
new situations as they arise. Because he has valued what is really valueless,
he will not generalize the lesson for fear of loss and sacrifice.

Manual for Teachers, pg. 10

At the Very Beginning

The human spirit is your specifically human dimension and contains abilities other creatures do not have. Every human is spiritual; in fact, spirit is the essence of being human. You have a body that may become ill; you have a psyche that may become disturbed. But the spirit is what you are. It is your healthy core.

- Joseph Fabry

This weekend we listened to a lecture on PBS by Wayne Dyer upon his book "The Power of Intention." Quite a few of his points during the talk excited us. One that I want to mention involved quantum physics; the very first second that you came into exist as a combination of the cells from your mother and father. This one cell defined all of your characteristics to the smallest detail! If you took that cell and searched it down to the molecular level with a powerful microscope, you would find that it was 99.9% empty space. The few particles that are in the space, if you looked at them with an even more powerful microscope, again, mostly empty space—nothing but Spirit. As you grew, you simply added more cells containing mostly nothing. And the particles that make up the cells are subject to change from particles to waves. When you pass this mortal veil, these cells will separate to form other substances. Thus, we go from spirit to spirit to spirit—with spirit defining us totally. Our challenge is to allow spirit to flow constantly to our awareness—that *all* things are similarly built and similarly subject to flex.

Now is our Source remembered, and therein we find our true Identity at last. Holy, indeed are we, because our Source can know no sin. And we who are His Sons are like each other, and alike to Him.

Workbook, pg. 424

88

Tough Lessons

A chip on the shoulder is too heavy a piece of baggage
to carry through life.

- John A. Hannah

You are an energy system and your feelings are broadcast out on a sort of energy loudspeaker. The stronger the feeling, the louder and farther they are distributed. The energy that you put out resonates with someone who matches with it in some way. For example, if you wake up feeling very angry toward yourself, someone might enter your day to trigger that anger. Maybe s/he will have an actual gun in the hand to physically end your life, also! Maybe a man will come in to strike you or an office worker may push your buttons in some other way. Your energy field actually represents a chip on your shoulder. If you look back on painful situations in your life, it should be possible to see that that was what happened, especially if the situation was a recent one. The "victim" actually sets the situation up to happen exactly the way it happened! There are no accidents!

If you have brown hair and someone tells you that they hate you because you have such ugly green hair, would you be offended and strike out, or would you be confused and amused? No offense would be accepted, because that "ugly green hair" button is not there and cannot be pushed!

Remove the buttons and chips. Remove the source of the energy. Forgiveness is the tool. When the source of the anger is completely released, the chip on the shoulder is gone and the buttons are no longer there to be pushed. Allow others to be as they have to be. Don't get sucked into other people's emotions. It's not that feelings are bad—but handle your feelings appropriately and don't be controlled by them. If you bury your feelings, they will come back to haunt you in some fashion. If your consciousness were clear, then no rapist would approach you and if one did, some "miracle" would happen to prevent the act. Practice forgiveness daily. Release the energy. Whenever you find yourself not peaceful, you are in a situation that calls for forgiveness and release.

I am not the victim of the world I see.

Workbook, pg. 94

All things work together for good. There are no exceptions except in the ego's judgment.

Text, pg. 65

When you meet anyone, remember it is a holy encounter. As you see him you will see yourself. As you treat him you will treat yourself. As you think of him you will think of yourself. Never forget this, for in him you will find yourself or lose yourself.

Text, pg. 142

If attack is not relinquished entirely, it is not relinquished at all.

Text, pg. 123

Our Deepest Fear

"Our deepest fear is not that we are inadequate.
Our deepest fear is that we are powerful beyond measure.
It is our light, not our darkness that most frightens us.
We ask ourselves, who am I to be brilliant, gorgeous, talented, and
fabulous?
Actually, who are you not to be? You are a child of God.
Your playing small doesn't serve the world.
There's nothing enlightened about shrinking so that other people
won't feel insecure around you.
We were born to make manifest the glory of God that is within us.
It's not just in some of us; it's in everyone.
And as we let our own light shine, we unconsciously give other
people permission to do the same."

- Marianne Williamson, quoted by Nelson Mandela

All fear is ultimately reducible to the basic misperception that you have the ability to usurp the power of God. Of course, you neither can nor have been able to do this. Here is the real basis for your escape from fear. The escape is brought about by your acceptance of the Atonement, which enables you to realize that your errors never really occurred. Only after the deep sleep fell upon Adam could he experience nightmares.

Text, pg. 18

Heaven Is Here

*The "kingdom of Heaven" is a condition of the heart – not
something that comes "upon the earth" or "after death."*

- Friedrich Nietzsche

Heaven is here, Heaven is now. There is no other place, there
is no other time. All of creation beckons you to experience
this time, this place, to let go of old ways of thinking, to let
yourself be united with Spirit. In Africa, they catch monkeys by
putting fruit in a box that has on one side a hole just large
enough for the monkey to put its hand in but too small for the
had to be pulled out while holding the fruit. The monkey cannot
make the connection in his mind that he would free himself by
releasing his hold on the fruit.

You are one with the Omniverse, with the All. You are a
Creator, awesome, radiant, and glorious to behold. All of Heaven
bows to you and places flowers below your feet. See the greater
oneness of All That Is—everywhere you look, everywhere you go.
Behold God in all, through all, everywhere present. Let the
illusions of this world fail to distract you from your quest to
return to Him. The "treasures" of this world are insignificant
when compared to His Glory and Truth. Take off the masks and
forget the games that children play, for you are beyond them now.
You have risen from your grave and are renewed, revitalized, and
born again in Spirit. Above all, just relax, for you don't have to *do*
anything. The Course says that we made the "separation" from
God when we forgot how to laugh. There is no busy-ness
required. Just be happy.

Together we will disappear into the Presence beyond the veil, not to be lost, but to be found, not to be seen but known. This is the journey's purpose, without which is the journey meaningless. Here is the peace of God, given to you eternally by Him. Here is the rest and quiet that you seek, the reason for the journey from the beginning. Heaven is the gift you owe your brother, the debt of gratitude you offer to the Son of God in thanks for what he is, and what his Father created him to be.

Text, pg. 424

What is heaven but a song of gratitude and love and praise by everything created to the Source of its creation?

Text, pg. 548

Accept the function that has been assigned to you in God's Own plan to show His Son that hell and Heaven are different, not the same. And that in Heaven They are all the same, without the differences which would have made a hell of Heaven and a heaven of hell, had such insanity been possible

Text, pg. 533

Addictions & Obsessions

*For many, negative thinking is a habit, which over time, becomes
an addiction... A lot of people suffer from this disease because
negative thinking is addictive to each of the Big Three -- the mind,
the body, and the emotions. If one doesn't get you,
the others are waiting in the wings.*

- Peter McWilliams

There are all kinds of addictions, some of which are socially
acceptable and some not. They are all basically the same.
When you are addicted to anything—whether it is food, drugs,
sex, alcohol, abuse, pornography, whatever—that addiction is an
indication that you consider yourself less than perfect, less than
happy, and are attempting to perfect yourself or make yourself
happy. Actually, the major thrust of humankind is towards God—
to find Him. Your deepest desire is to have Him love you again,
and to love yourself again. It motivates your activities,
unconscious though it may be. You are looking out there in the
world for something to replace the function of God in your life.
However, there *is* nothing in the world that can even come close
to taking God's place. God *is* your life, the Spirit of your days and
nights here on earth. You were created in His Image.

You have raised images to take His place in the form of these
things. There is a "hole" in your psyches that tells you that you
are incomplete without God, but you have forgotten that and
attempt to fill up that "hole" with something physical. You are
searching outside of yourself for your completion and any search
outside of yourself is doomed to failure because, in actuality,
there *is* nothing outside of yourself. Everything "out there" is a
function of your interpretation, of your perception filters, and of
your judgments towards others and especially toward yourself.
You make your universe *exactly* the way it is through your
thoughts. Your decisions are motivated by your mis-
interpretations and judgments. You are often your worst enemy,
with your judgments of how "bad" you are.

When you care enough about yourself, no matter what the
addiction, that addiction will fade away. You are bigger you're
your addictions, obsessions, and habits! Humankind has a basic

fear of God's punishment for having usurped His Power in its lives. They decide that they are in charge; that they know what is right for them better than God does, so the ego assists them in thinking they are separated from God. **E.G.O.** is an acronym for **E**asing **G**od **O**ut. The ego doesn't want God in your life; it wants to be in charge. Any attempt on your part to include God meets with stiff resistance. The ego is a crafty thing, being a part of your thought system. It finds ways to distract you, to make you "forget," to delay you, and to lead you down other paths that seem to have the same end for which you are searching.

God loves you and you are worthy of being loved. There is no one more worthy than you are, no matter what your judgment of yourself is, or how much you have "sinned." Seek for nothing outside of yourself or you will be setting yourself up for failure and disappointment. All that you need is within you. All that you can change is only changeable through your thinking. Stinking thinking is what brings about addictions and obsessions in the first place. If you change your thinking, you change your life.

I sought for many things, and found despair. Now do I seek
but one, for in that one is all I need, and only what I need.
All that I sought before I needed not, and did not even want.
My only need I did not recognize. But now I see that I need
only truth. In that all needs are satisfied, all cravings end,
all hopes are finally fulfilled and dreams are gone. Now have I
everything that I could need. Now have I everything
that I could want. And now at last I find myself at peace.

Workbook, pg. 420

Guilt is a sure sign that your thinking is unnatural.

Text, pg. 84

Addictions & Obsessions,
Part B

People spend a lifetime searching for happiness; looking for peace.
They chase idle dreams, addictions, religions, even other people,
hoping to fill the emptiness that plagues them. The irony is the only
place they ever needed to search was within.

- Romana L. Anderson

Take the case of Bill, who is addicted to drugs. Bill had to make a choice whether or not to take that first step. He can find all kinds of excuses as to why, but the knowledge of the possibility of addiction and danger was there all the time. He simply chose to do it. What caused him to take the first step? He was subconsciously looking for joy and happiness. He was looking for an experience of God. He had been disappointed by life and wanted escape, so he advanced one more step. What motivated this? He found what he was looking for, he thought, a substitute, at least, but that turned out not to be a consistent feeling, so he upped the dosage. And so it continues. Other addictions take place in similar ways. Food, for example, very definitely fills a "hole," It is easy to become addicted to it because you cannot turn your back on it completely.

Obsessions are similar to addictions in that they are something you use to distract you from seriously searching for God. Business, family, and relationships, are some of the many things that can become obsessions. Workaholics are obsessed with "success." Failure is not an option for them. To the parent who is obsessed with his/her family, in a codependent relationship with their families, their entire being and identity is involved in the family.

It seems to be "hard" to change. Where do you start? How do you change your thinking? The correction takes place in mini-steps, forming habits that have a gradual rebuilding effect. Practicing remaining conscious and aware increasingly throughout the day, week, and month. Being in the "now" is an important tool, because of the tendency to let the thinking of the world take over your thoughts and actions. Minute by minute, day by day, even second by second, choices are made. There will be tendencies to go unconscious, temptations, forgetfulness, and failure to deal with along the way. If you get caught by any of these, come back to center; ask for help from Spirit to forgive yourself and to get back on the path. This is your opportunity to give over the addiction to Holy Spirit, the Divine Thought Adjuster, to have your "evil" thoughts taken from you. They may have served you at one time, but they don't serve any more—you don't need them any more.

Remember this—you are not, and never could be, victims of any outside force in your life. You are a Master! You are in charge of your life! You are responsible. This is not to make you feel guilty for any conditions you observe in your life, but to help you realize that your thoughts, your decisions, build your lives step by step, and brick by brick. The addictions and obsessions that you are facing are simply opportunities for you to realize that you are a powerful being of light and capable of healing yourself.

Have you really considered how many opportunities you have had to gladden yourself, and how many of them you have refused? There is no limit to the power of a Son of God, but he can limit the expression of his power as much as he chooses.

Text, pg. 64

The ego analyzes; the Holy Spirit accepts... The ego believes that power, understanding and truth lie in separation, and to establish this belief it must attack. Unaware that the belief cannot be established, and obsessed with the conviction that separation is salvation, the ego attacks everything it perceives by breaking it into small, disconnected parts, without meaningful relationships and therefore without meaning.

Text, pg. 205

I Wish You

"I wish you enough sun to keep your attitude bright.
I wish you enough rain to appreciate the sun more.
I wish you enough happiness to keep your spirit alive.
I wish you enough pain so that
the smallest joys in life appear much bigger.
I wish you enough gain to satisfy your wanting.
I wish you enough loss to appreciate all that you possess.
I wish you enough 'Hello's'
to get you through the final 'Good-bye.'"

- Bob Perks

What a wonderful quote! This is an example of love that looks to the Soul of the friend or loved one. The author does not wish an easy and carefree life with all needs met and no troubles at all. Instead, he sees that some pain and troubles are of benefit. They help one to grow. Have you been praying to have all your troubles removed from you without realizing the big picture of God's Love for you? Have you been regretting the rainy days, wishing that the sun would always shine? Think again!

Give faith to your brother, for faith and hope and mercy are yours to give.
Into the hands that give, the gift is given. Look on your brother, and see in
him the gift of God you would receive. Behold the gift of freedom that I gave
the Holy Spirit for you. And be you and your brother free together,
as you offer to the Holy Spirit this same gift.

Text, pg. 423

Love

I think the biggest disease this world suffers from...is people feeling unloved.

- Diana, Princess of Wales

Love is the great healing force; love is all there is. Love cannot be really defined—you only limit it by trying. It is the glue that holds this world together. Love never attacks, never grieves, and never feels lonely. Love binds together and never separates. Love is of God and goes with you wherever you go. Love is not selfish, but is always kind; love is always returned to you. Release any barriers you have built to your awareness of love's presence a little at a time. You do not have to *try* to love, for love happens naturally. Remember that no effort is required in nature. A bird doesn't have to try to fly; he just does. Just *be* love, for love is all that you are and all that you can be, anyway. You have the opportunity to teach hatred, bigotry and selfishness, but teach only love and that love will be returned and strengthened in yourself. Send love ahead of you to places that you are going to prepare the way and make smooth the journey.

Love unconditionally, placing no responsibilities upon those who receive your love. Unconditional love is love without a hook in it, allowing a person to be as he/she has to be, not as you would have them be. If you love someone for what they have to give to you, you love selfishly. This is the Holy Relationship from **A Course in Miracles**. Your love, given freely, falls upon all the human family and blesses the world.

Your task is not to seek for love, but merely to seek and find all the barriers within yourself that you have built against it. It is not necessary to seek for what is true, but it is necessary to seek for what is false.

Text, pg. 338

Each Moment

Each moment of Love,
Each moment of giving,
Each moment of Joy
Is a moment of living.
Each moment of fear,
Each moment of lying,
Each moment of resentment
Is a moment of dying.
All our moments add together,
Like the digits in a sum
And the answer tells us plainly
Whether Heaven or Hell shall come.

- Lord Cecil Martin

Each moment is precious. Do not spend it in the past. The past is gone. What was painful in it was painful enough at the time without torturing yourself with it again, over and over. There was a lady whose car broke down. A man stopped to ostensibly help her, but instead attacked her with a knife and left her for dead. She managed to crawl to a house where another man, instead of helping her, raped her repeatedly. She managed to make it through these times, though, and today is a Religious Science minister. When a friend asked her why she didn't talk about these attacks, she told him that those men had her in their possession for long enough. They weren't going to take over her mind now. Value your precious moments and don't be held prisoner to the past!

The emphasis of this course always remains the same; it is at this moment that complete salvation is offered you, and it is at this moment that you can accept it. This is still your one responsibility. Atonement might be equated with total escape from the past and total lack of interest in the future. Heaven is here. There is nowhere else. Heaven is now. There is no other time.

Manual for Teachers, pg. 61

Each day a thousand treasures come to me with every passing moment. I am blessed with gifts throughout the day, in value far beyond all things of which I can conceive. A brother smiles upon another, and my heart is gladdened. Someone speaks a word of gratitude or mercy, and my mind receives this gift and takes it as its own. And everyone who finds the way to God becomes my savior, pointing out the way to me, and giving me his certainty that what he learned is surely mine as well.

Workbook, pg. 458

Prayer

Our God, which art our winged self,
It is Thy Will in us that willeth.
It is Thy Desire in us that desireth.
It is Thy urge in us that would turn our nights,
Which are thine, into days which are thine, also.
We cannot ask thee for aught,
For Thou knowest our needs before they are born in us.
Thou art our need, and in giving us more of Thyself,
Thou givest us all.

- Kahlil Gibran, *The Prophet*

Mother, Father, God:
My prayer is that I become more and more aware of my Sonship to You, that I accept, not just in my head, but in my heart and my total awareness, my greatness and my holiness. I pray that I find the strength to become alert to all judgments and unforgiving thoughts, and that I practice true forgiveness of all my brothers and especially of myself. I would allow the presence of Christ awareness of the true nature of all creation to be ever uppermost in my life. Dropping all pretenses, fears and jealousies, I pray that I may know that my will is one with Your Will, that there is nothing that I cannot do, and that I am the light of the world in truth. I further pray that I may begin to release this world and live more and more in Heaven, holding Your Hand, trusting Your Plan for me, risking all that this world holds for the greater glory of love. Thank you, Amen.

God's will for you is perfect happiness. Why should you choose to go against His Will? The part that He has saved for you to take in working out His plan is given you that you might be restored to what He wills. This part is as essential to His plan as to your happiness.

Workbook, pg. 180

It is quite possible to listen to God's Voice all through the day without interrupting your regular activities in any way. The part of your mind in which truth abides is in constant communication with God, whether you are aware of it or not.

Workbook, pg. 78

You first forgive, then pray, and you are healed. Your prayer has risen up and called to God, Who hears and answers. You have understood that you forgive and pray but for yourself. And in this understanding you are healed. In prayer you have united with your Source, and understood that you have never left. This level cannot be attained until there is no hatred in your heart, and no desire to attack the Son of God.

Song of Prayer, pg. S-3.IV.4

What You Resist

"What is needed, rather than running away or controlling or suppressing or any other resistance, is understanding fear; that means, watch it, learn about it, come directly into contact with it. We are to learn about fear not how to escape from it."

- Jiddu Krishnamurti

What you resist, persists: so the saying goes, and it is certainly true! Remember that everything is composed of energy. The energy of resistance becomes an energy of attraction, a magnetic force. No matter what seems to be facing you—large or small—in this world, you can find another way of looking at it. There will be a way around, a way through, or a benefit that was unexpected in it. If you are getting a shot, become one with the needle and accept the small pain involved. If you are stuck in traffic, use the time to reflect, to listen to a tape or CD, or to simply sit there and relax and reflect, making it a time of peace rather than of anger and impatience. If you, like Roosevelt, are facing a major situation, you can find a way to go *through* it, rather than be defeated by it.

The universe is looking for ways to support you, rather than attacking you. History is filled with those who have overcome. Every biography that is written contains a "low" time in the person's life—a time of loss, or death of a loved one, or bankruptcy, or failure at one effort or another. Those people were not better than you are, and you are not less than they were. They used a situation like a pole-vaulter uses his pole—to impel them over the obstacle. They became MORE determined by failure, rather than less. Of course, for everyone who succeeded, there are thousands who fail. All events and things in this universe are energy, and energy is something with which you can work. Miracles can happen, no matter how dark the illusion appears. Find another perception. Look at it differently. Make a "what's so" into a "so what." Turn the other cheek. Expand; don't contract. Be happy and joy-filled always.

When you have learned how to decide with God, all decisions become as easy and as right as breathing. There is no effort, and you will be fed as gently as if you were being carried down a quiet path in summer.

Text, pg. 280

Everyone here has entered darkness, yet no one has entered it alone. Nor need he stay more than an instant. For he has come with Heaven's Help within Him, ready to lead him out of darkness into light at any time. The time he chooses can be any time; for help is there, awaiting but his choice. And when he chooses to avail himself of what is given him, then will he see each situation that he thought before was means to justify his anger turned into an event that justifies his love. He will hear plainly that the calls to war he heard before are really calls to peace.

Text, pg. 524

The World Outside My Door

The world outside my door
Is brought to me in part
By its quiet desperation
And its hunger for relief

The world outside my door
Is brought to me in part
By a grant of my perception
Loosely based on my belief

I'm challenged to wrestle the illusions
Of everything I think that I should be
Now I've placed these goals before me
Somewhere in the distance
Now they keep me running to be free

It's a good day when I win
Over the drama I've created
When I can stand my ground at least
And it's a bad day when I'm sucked into the vortex of the dream
Dragged down to the belly of the beast

In the passing of the days
In the passing of my judgment
In the passing of all these things I do
In the rising and the falling
You know nothing really changes
Nothing changes but my point of view

(Chorus)
I am awakening again, awakening
From the spell that I've been under
I am awakening again, awakening
And I'm opening the kingdom
With this tiny key of wonder
Awakening again.

Weaving through the many ways
I choose to see the world
As I try to hold it in my hand
There is the steady constant dream
Of the way it really is
The mystery is unfolding
Of the plan

With the shift in my awareness
I crack the noise and drink the silence
Pierce the veil and touch the truth
And shed my skin

In the dominion of the moment
I am timeless and in the stillness
I am lifted from the fullness
From within

(Chorus)

I look at my possessions
They seem funny to me now
All these things I collect to mark my space
Hey I must have thought these things
That just clutter up my room
Could define me and hold me to this place

Now I close my eyes and I'm halfway home
So much more than I can see
I arrive at the place
I've always been,
Free of where I think I ought to be

(Chorus)

Deeper than the voices
that say time is running out
Against the ego's insatiable demands
Deeper than the part of me that struggles to control
The world that won't respond to my commands

Deep in the stillness
In the hush of the silence
I hear the wordless whisper of peace
It is here that I remember
Who I am, it is here I am released

(Alternate version of chorus)
I am awakening again, awakening
And I'm standing in the presence
I am awakening again, awakening
And I'm connected to all there is
Through my acceptance.
Awakening again.

There is wisdom in not knowing
There is freedom in release
There is power in surrender to the Source
There's a sailing ship of wonder
Upon an ocean that's unfolding
And it's charting an unknown course

And there's a gift that I've been given
That I know I must give back
Something I cannot deny
The fact is I'm unique
Just like everybody else
Giving back to the infinite supply

(Chorus)

- Lyrics by Ed Munter from **"Awakening Again"**

You are not yet awake, but you can learn how to awaken. Very simply, the Holy Spirit teaches you to awaken others. As you see them waken you will learn what waking means, and because you have chosen to wake them, their gratitude and their appreciation of what you have given them will teach you its value. They will become the witnesses to your reality, as you were created witness to God's.

Text, pg. 174

We walk together on the way to quietness that is the gift of God. Hold me dear, for what except your brothers can you need? We will restore to you the peace of mind that we must find together. The Holy Spirit will teach you to awaken unto us and to yourself.

Text, pg. 257

Identity

*Joy, rather than happiness, is the goal of life, for joy is the emotion
which accompanies our fulfilling our natures as human beings.
It is based on the experience of one's identity as
a being of worth and dignity.*

- Rollo May

What is your identity? What do you identify with? Are you your body? What is it without you? Are you identified in your mind with your wife or husband? Are you identified with your children? Your job? Your car? Your weight? The color of your skin? Your sex? Who are you, really? You might have divided your identity among several of these. Have you divided yourself up until there is nothing left? Are you confused and torn?

In the busy-ness of the world you wear many masks and often change your personality to match the circumstances. You have compartmentalized yourself and put a label on each compartment. Along with the compartments there are expectations of yourself and others and judgments of performance regarding those expectations. Is it any wonder that you get depressed and angry? You can't meet all of your high expectations in every area of life, and failure in one area can't help but to reflect in other areas. For example, a man has a family that consists of a wife and three children. He is obliged to maintain the house and the yard, perform well on the job, communicate well with his family, and many others. He is a citizen of a community, a town or city, a state, a country, and the world. All of these are also pressing for his attention. He may be a member of a church or other spiritual group, a club. The wife's life is similarly divided, and sometimes even more so, if she has a job, takes care of the meals and cleaning, and is obligated to take the largest part of raising the children.

What you want out of life is also compartmentalized and confused. Your life is focused on the physical and the temporary. Your desires often conflict with those in other areas or with other people's desire that are close to you. When do you get a chance to fulfill your own deepest desires, whatever they may be? When the activity gets too intense and the feelings of resentment have grown to their ultimate point, you find that marriages often fail and families break apart upon the shoals of the stressful life you lead. Many break away from this kind of life and find comfort in being homeless.

This paints a pretty dismal picture of life, in the western world, especially. You have missed the boat. You are trying to find happiness but at the same time your search for happiness leads you around in circles as you chase one rabbit after another on the racetrack. At some point a decision has to be made to get back to the basics, back to the center, back to the important things of life—back to God. It does not matter what you name it— call it God, Jesus, Allah, Buddha, Jeshua, or Higher Self. It does not matter. With God, all things are possible. With God, you have strength indefatigable. With God, you have guidance and peace. In God, you find joy everlasting in the midst of the chaos of this illusionary world. In God, you find the answers to your confusion, depression, and questions. In God, you find what you truly want.

Stop, Look, & Listen! The world goes by so fast that sometimes it is a healthy move to just stop and sit down on a park bench, for instance, and watch. Watch the children, the animals, and just relax for a while each week. Observe. Separate yourself from the world and be an observer of the world. Observe all the chaos and insanity, the pain and terror that goes on and be in the world but not caught up in it. You cannot correct an error at the level of the error. You cannot help the world while trapped within its illusions.

The way to God is through forgiveness here. There is no other way.

Workbook, pg. 422

In reality you are perfectly unaffected by all expressions of lack of love. These can be from yourself and others, from yourself to others, or from others to you. Peace is an attribute in you. You cannot find it outside.

Text, pg. 18

Need Nothing

"Need nothing. Desire everything. Accept what shows up."
- Neale Donald Walsch, *Conversations with God*

The average man or woman on the street goes from need to need. They have a wish list of things that would make them happy. What is on your list? What would make you happy? If you won the lottery? What would complete you and fulfill your innermost or most shallow desires —a car, a house, or the perfect mate? When/if you achieve one of these wants, what do you feel? Happy? For how long? In your wants, you are expressing a need for something that seems to be lacking in your life. You are searching for completion, and that completion can only be fulfilled by a renewal of your sacred relationship with Spirit. When you take the steps necessary to raise your awareness of Spirit, then things and people will be attracted to you. Desire is a step higher than need, for desire means "of the Father," and when you seek—not for fulfillment—for joy, then you are in line with Spirit.

Nothing in this world really has to happen in order to have miracles occur in your life. A simple change in perspective, a new outlook, a new thought, a new idea, is all that is required. You need do nothing! The whole process, (the bottom line), is reduced to one of staying in the now moment, letting go of the old and claiming your strength *in God, loving God, and having faith in His Love for you.*

Deep within you is everything that is perfect, ready to radiate through you and out into the world.

Workbook, pg. 63

Tragedies

God has marvelous ways of taking our worst tragedies and turning them into His most glorious triumphs.

- Joseph Stowall

The Course tells us to be vigilant for God and His kingdom. Be vigilant in the face of earthquakes, tsunamis, tornadoes, floods, and whatever "tragedies" that will befall the world. See beyond the pain, the fear, and the seeming death to the Truth that lies beyond, through, and over this illusion that you are experiencing in this world. Hold to your faith in the Love of God, Who would never visit such things upon His Beloved Sons. What you fear most comes upon you, so replace fear thoughts with loving thoughts, not believing the messages your eyes and ears give you.

This is a tough lesson, but it is made tough because all of us are so dependent on our eyes for information—but our eyes see only the illusion. This world is not real. It is a mirror of the sum of man's thought, judgment, and perceptions, projected upon space. The trick is to remember that the world and everything in it is not real, no matter how "real" or "terrible" or "wonderful" it appears.

Do not feel worried about the world; do not be concerned about the things you see in the world to the point where you get carried away. Rise above the battleground and see what God sees. Take care of your neighbor, the poor, the helpless, those in pain, but know at the same time that they are Children of God. Their "plight" is serving them in ways we can never judge. Only God can judge truly. *Be ye **in** the world, but not **of** it!*

The Holy Spirit guides you into life eternal, but you must relinquish your investment in death or you will not see life, though it is all around you.

Text, pg. 225

Stress

Your body is an amazing creation, capable of performing great wonders, but you can destroy that miraculous machine's potential with an overdose of stress.

- Harry J. Johnson

A lecturer, when explaining stress management to an audience, raised a glass of water and asked, "how heavy is this glass of water?" Answers called out ranged from 20 grams to 500 grams. The lecturer replied, "The absolute weight doesn't matter. It depends on how long you try to hold it.

"If I hold it for a minute, that's not a problem. If I hold it for an hour, I'll have an ache in my right arm. If I hold it for a day, you'll have to call an ambulance. In each case, it's the same weight, but the longer I hold it, the heavier it becomes."

He continued, "And that's the way it is with stress management. If we carry our burdens all the time, sooner or later, as the burden becomes increasingly heavy, we won't be able to carry on. As with the glass of water, you have to put it down for a while and rest before holding it again. When we're refreshed, we can carry on with the burden.

"So, before you return home tonight, put the burden of work down. Don't carry it home. You can pick it up tomorrow. Whatever burden you are carrying now, put them down for a moment if you can. Relax; pick them up later after you've rested. Life is short. Enjoy it!"

And then he shared these 17 suggestions about dealing with the burdens of life:

1. Accept that some days you're the pigeon and some days you're the statue.

2. Always keep your words soft and sweet, just in case you have to eat them.

3. Always read stuff that will make you look good if you die in the middle of it.

4. Drive carefully. It's not only cars that can be recalled by their maker.

5. If you can't be kind, at least have the decency to be vague.

6. If you lend someone $20 and never see that person again, it was probably worth it.

7. Never buy a car you can't push.

8. Never put both feet in your mouth at the same time, because then you won't have a leg to stand on.

9. Nobody cares if you can't dance well. Just get up and dance.

10. Since it's the early worm that gets eaten by the bird, sleep late.

11. The second mouse gets the cheese (in a mousetrap).

12. When everything's coming your way, you're in the wrong lane.

13. Birthdays are good for you: the more you have, the longer you live.

14. You may be only one person in the world, but you may also be the world to one person.

15. A truly happy person is one who can enjoy the scenery on a detour.

16. Some mistakes are too much fun to only make once.

17. We could learn a lot from crayons. Some are sharp, some are pretty and some are dull. Some have weird names, and all are different colors, but they all have to live in the same box.

> \- From email—author unknown.

You have an opportunity to be happy, regardless of what is happening in your life. Choose once again.

Do you prefer that you be right or happy?

Text, pg. 617

Celebrate!

"Life has meaning only in the struggle. Triumph or defeat is in the hands of the Gods. So let us celebrate the struggle!"

- Swahili Warrior Song

Celebrate! Celebrate your life just the way it is, for it is perfect. You are power-filled. In alignment with Spirit you can create miracles. By changing your perception, you create miracles. All power and glory are yours *right now*. Claim it, *be* it. Don't play small any more. You are a Child of God, in whom He is well pleased. God does not see your humanness, your failures. He sees only the perfect Child He created perfect, whole, and complete. So let your judgments of yourself and others go. You are God also, Spirit in human form. Situations and conditions are fluid; by changing your perspective they can easily and effortlessly change. Constantly align with Spirit and step out on faith.

Look at your life right now. No matter what it looks like, you have out-pictured your consciousness upon it. You have drawn people, conditions, and situations to you. If the people, conditions, and situations don't serve you, start to raise your consciousness. How? Just by knowing that all of these things are illusions—the observer is the participant in the dream—you can change the dream by changing your mind about it.

For example, a teacher of mine had been very angry with his father for 40 years. When he finally discussed his anger with his sibling, he found an entirely new way of perceiving the situation that he had never considered. Like a light bulb coming on in the dark the anger of 40 years was undone and he was able to forgive his father and himself.

Be still and be with God. Let Him guide you. Give your challenges over to Holy Spirit. Know that you can go through each day holding the Hand of Christ. The universe is on your side!! Step out on faith. All things are of God and His Love blesses you.

*What is Heaven but a song of gratitude and love and praise
by everything created to the Source of its creation?*

Text, pg. 548

*There is a light in you the world cannot give. Yet you can give it, as it was
given you. And as you give it, it shines forth to call you from the world and
follow it. For this light will attract you as nothing in this world can do.
And you will lay aside this world and find another. This other world is
bright with love which you have given it. And here everything will remind
you of your Father and His Holy Son. Light is unlimited and
spreads across this world in quiet joy.*

Text, pg. 253

*You have the right to all the universe; to perfect peace, complete deliverance
from all effects of sin, and to the life eternal, joyous and complete
in every way, as God appointed for His holy Son.*

Text, pg. 538

The Insanity
Of the World

*"Insanity is doing the same thing in the same way
and expecting a different outcome".*

- Chinese Proverb

The insanity of the world is much on my mind lately. The inhumanity of mankind to all aspects of the rest of humanity, to the world is weighing heavily upon me. I suspect that sometimes it is the same with you, so I thought I would share my feelings and my thoughts with you. I know that the Course says that this is all an illusion, and on a mind level, I know that this is true, but I see a TV show or read a book and my senses are bombarded with feelings of helplessness towards those who are seemingly being abused, tortured, or plundered in many ways. I don't think that not watching TV or not reading books is necessarily the answer. The answer is in my heart, mind, and emotions.

What I keep coming back to, albeit somewhat late at times, is that the victims and the victimizers are in a dance—a dance in which both have agreed to participate on some unconscious level. My going out to pull them out of their misery only means that I am holding the illusion as real, making their pain more intense, and continuing the misery for others.

There is a story about a little Angel who could not keep her candle lit because of the tears of those who were left behind, weeping for themselves when they thought they were weeping for her.

Empathy is called forth; love is called forth. Love IS the answer to all questions. This doesn't mean that I can't help, can't give them a shoulder to cry on, can't be there for them to share their pain, but I don't choose to let them pull me down to the point where I can't see the higher truth for them and myself. I am no good to anyone operating from the level upon which they see themselves as lost and alone.

If I go into a hospital room and see a sick person, I leave until I can go back in and see a loved and beautiful Child of God regardless of the seeming "reality" of the situation.

Love is what you come for,
Love is what you are.
Love is where you're going.
Love is all there is!

Grace is acceptance of the Love of God within a world of seeming hate and fear. By grace alone the hate and fear are gone, for grace represents a state so opposite of everything the world contains, that those whose minds are lighted by the gift of grace can not believe the world of fear is real.

Workbook, pg. 323

Glory is God's gift to you, because that is what He is. See this glory everywhere to remember what you are.

Text, pg. 143

Honesty

The true measure of life is not length, but honesty.

- John Lyly

What are the things that you are dishonest about? What are the small larcenies, the "little white" lies? Are you honest with your income taxes? Do you take pencils, paper clips, notebooks, and copy machine paper home? Do you abuse the company equipment—phones, copy machines, fax machines? Do you exceed the speed limit on the highway? The "small" things are the ones that you hide and build such a burden of guilt on conscious and subconscious levels.

What if you accidentally broke something and someone else got blamed for it? Would you confess? If you find a billfold in a store, do you make every effort to turn it over to the owner and leave the money intact? What if you opened your car door in a parking lot and the wind jerked it out of your grip and damaged an automobile parked next to you, would you try to find the person or at least leave a note with your phone number? What are your limits on honesty? Is it a dollar price? Is it an embarrassment level, claiming an "honest" mistake—you "accidentally" picked it up and put it in your pocket? Have you ever manipulated some one else into doing something that is a risk but would benefit you? Are you tempted to take something left lying there unattended? If someone asks for your opinion, do you skate around the issue or tell them what you think they want to hear? What are the other ways that you find yourself saying or doing something that is less than honest? What is so wrong about exceeding the speed limit, anyway? Everyone does it!

Christ said to give unto Caesar the things that are Caesar's and to God that which is God's. Man's rules are the contract under which you live while on this planet. These are some of the ways that you sell yourself short by being dishonest in one way or another in order to gain in some fashion. Maybe your parents didn't set such a good example—you learned dishonesty at their knees. Maybe the reason for these dishonest activities is a lack of self-esteem—you consider yourself as "only human." Maybe it's too much trouble to do the "right" thing. Maybe it will cost you big bucks to repair that car door that you damaged. Maybe you are just taking the "easy" way, capitulating to temptation, rather than being a responsible adult who is compassionate with himself and others. Maybe it is time to evaluate your values, your compassion for others, and changing the way you look at issues such as these. Now is the time to start living love in all ways. Thinking and talking one way and then behaving another way is not being honest to your higher truth.

From your holy relationship truth proclaims the truth, and love looks on itself. Salvation flows from deep within the home you offered to my Father and to me. And we are there together, in the quiet communion in which the Father and the Son are joined. O come ye faithful to the holy union of the Father and the Son in you!

Text, pg. 413

…when a situation has been dedicated wholly to truth, peace is inevitable.

Text, pg. 398

Truth can only be experienced. It cannot be described and it cannot be explained…Truth will dawn upon you of itself.

Text, pg. 150

The Prodigal Son

Evil, and evil spirits, devils and devil possession, are the outgrowth of man's inadequate consciousness of God. We must avoid thinking of evil as a thing in itself-a force that works against man or, against God, if you will.

- Eric Butterworth

The example of the prodigal son is a very enlightening story. When you stray from your Father's Home, the Love of God is still there and you will be welcomed back with great rejoicing and you will be stronger for the experience. If you have been asleep to your oneness with God, you are in the midst of a nightmare. You are living in a world made of illusions and madness. There is no evil, no bad, no wrong. Evil, bad, and wrong cannot exist because God did not create them. God does not know evil, bad, and sin. They are foreign to the nature of God. Evil is "live" spelled backward, so an "evil" person is living life backwards from the way it was intended.

You have created a God that is in your own likeness, not the other way around. You made your ego because you perceived yourself as separated and alone. *A Course in Miracles* tells us that man's perception of separation from God began at the moment that His Son forgot how to laugh. The idea of separation from takes the form of sickness, disease, loss, sin, loneliness, failure, insanity, illusions, pain, fear, and so many others. All of the "troubles" in this world can be traced back to it

You cannot understand how much your Father loves you, for there is no parallel in your experience of the world to help you understand it. There is nothing on earth with which it can compare, and nothing you have ever felt apart from Him resembles it ever so faintly.

Text, pg. 281

Taking the
Easy Way Out

Insanity: doing the same thing over and over again and expecting different results.

Albert Einstein

In this day of instant this, instant that, instant everything, hurry up, bottom line world, many people find themselves with a lot of stress and the easy way to relieve that stress is to try to find shortcuts. In the hurry and scurry daily rush, the individual can be stressed out even more when instant relief is not at hand. This works in metaphysics, also. Once the mind is open to new ways of thinking and healing, impatience for enlightenment often creeps in. There is a tendency to backslide in consciousness upon entering the metaphysical path because the individual tends to focus on what's wrong, rather than what's right. Also, people are startled to find that as they grow, their world seems to fall apart, relationships are drastically altered, and elements of their lives are rearranged. This can be most disconcerting. Hold on for the roller coaster ride! Taking the easy way involves omitting the practices that so deepen the daily existence—meditations, readings, classes, and seminars. One can't keep on doing things the same way and expect different results: that is the definition for insanity. The paradigm in the fourth dimension is in community, togetherness, group activities, etc., so in order to maximize the spiritual quest; one would seek out and participate in as many of these as possible.

The mind that serves the Holy Spirit is unlimited forever, in all ways, beyond the laws of time and space, unbound by any preconceptions, and with strength and power to do whatever it is asked.

Workbook, pg. 382

Faith

*"Faith is an oasis in the heart which will never be reached
by the caravan of thinking."*

- Kahlil Gibran, *Sand & Foam*

This is a Universe of infinite abundance: spiritual, mental, and physical. This Bounty of Spirit, this Allness of Good, is limitless and can never be exhausted or depleted. This infinite Bounty of Spirit is the birthright of every human. I am a child of God, created as a finite expression of God. Thus, I am heir to all the Good there is, simply because of who I am. "How do I know if it is God who is speaking to me?" Haven't you wondered at times? It's all about faith. I have been in many workshops where this question was raised. It's different for everyone, but when you hear God's Voice, you know!

First, you must hear the message. Listen! Meditate! It sometimes helps to learn to meditate through taking classes; meditating in a group is especially helpful. I like to think of meditating as going to the well to drink from God's Wisdom and Love. Clear the thousands of self-talk messages going through your head. Look honestly and deeply for the God within, and ask to hear His voice above the voice of your own ego, which speaks so loudly. Listen for what God's response to you may be, for what God's needs of you might be, God's hopes and desires for you—for that small, still voice. The indwelling God is real, and is longing for you to discover the signs and wisdom of His presence within you. Listen, and you will hear.

Have as much faith that God is within you and supporting you as you have faith in gravity, electricity; and that the sun will rise each day. Develop a relationship with the Presence of God within through meditation. Once a deep realization of God within, as you, having faith is like trusting the law of gravity. It just is, Well, God just is. All you have to do is relax and let God express, to step out on that limb—not hoping, but *knowing* that God protects you, nourishes you, if only you allow Him to do so. When confronted with alternatives, go inside in meditation and visualize yourself in each of these situations. Talk with people whom you trust to be honest and truthful, but test their answers by your "gut feeling." Sometimes the direction in which God leads you does not make any sense to the intellectual mind. Sometimes it comes in a series of "nudges," but it sometimes takes the application of the proverbial "2x4 cosmic hammer" until you "get" it.

Second, the writer of First John advises you to, "...test the spirits to see whether they be of God." (*I John 4:1*). The test is finding the Truth—*knowing* that God is real, and *knowing* your oneness with It. God is the God of Truth—all kinds of Truth. For example, trust that God wouldn't send you to Africa to care for the poor in spirit if you wouldn't choose that for yourself. God wouldn't ask you to give everything you have away if you wouldn't choose to do so. The scripture says if you seek you will find, and if you knock the door will be opened. The most difficult part is having the courage to move forward through the open door. Sometimes moving forward is simply taking one tiny step and then remaining open to the possibility of taking another. However, you can't really make a "bad" step; you might want to rethink, or go in a different direction after the first step, though. Just take a deep breath, let go of the branch to which you are desperately clinging and swing through to catch the other branch—you can't go forward while hanging on! Don't be afraid any longer, but believe. Everything is possible to the one who believes. God requires belief and trust in moments of human weakness, but faith is what makes you strong—you greatly increase spiritual growth when you step out on faith. Your faith will grow in proportion to the leaps of faith that you take.

Third, listen to the voice of your conscience, your sense of moral responsibility. The ego, though, loves to confuse and confound. One way of judging right from wrong is to ask the question, "How would I feel if every person in the world practiced the same code of ethics that I do?" A word of caution here: your conscience may not always lead you to do the right thing. The most heinous crimes against humanity have been committed in the name of conscience and religion. You have the capacity for moral decision-making, and your challenge is to cultivate the highest code of ethics.

Fourth, beware the voice of tradition or culture (group thought) around you speaking to you, rather than an authentic Word from God. The difference is not always easy to determine because you are bombarded with messages from many sources. The cultural messages scream from billboards and television screens, from parents and siblings, from everywhere. Determining which is true requires you to develop a strong sense of spirituality. The deeper you go on your own spiritual search, the easier it is to hear the divine message. This search involves a lifetime commitment. The joy of the journey into the mind of God is that more and more you discover what God wants you to do with your life. You *are* being addressed. God is waiting for your response.

Nothing can prevail against a Son of God who commends his spirit into the Hands of his Father.

Text, pg. 39

When you have learned how to decide with God, all decisions become as easy and as right as breathing. There is no effort, and you will be fed as gently as if your were being carried down a quiet path in summer.

Text, pg. 280

No evidence will convince you of the truth of what you do not want.

Text, pg. 333

The children God are entitled to the perfect comfort that comes from perfect trust. Until they achieve this, they waste themselves and their true creative powers on useless attempts to make themselves more comfortable by inappropriate means.

Text, pg. 22

The Journey

*"What you are afraid to do is a clear indicator
of the next thing you need to do."*
                    - Dr. Ernest Holmes, *The Science of Mind*

The old adage "Time flies when you're having fun" is true, but when you are on a vacation, doesn't it seem like it passed by so rapidly that you didn't get a chance to really enjoy it? Try to take one moment at a time—one beautiful, glorious moment at a time. The destination is not the important thing. The importance lies in the journey, the time spent before and after reaching the destination. It doesn't matter if the trip is an actual physical trip, or just a period of time. When you anticipate what lies ahead so much that you miss the trip to get there, you lose the moments in between the decision to make the trip and the arrival at the destination. If you also form an opinion about what is supposed to happen at the end of the trip, you often face disappointment and depression. If you are open to the perfect activity of a loving and caring God, you can accept the outcome knowing that your highest and best good has been served. You don't need to understand it; you just need to know that a blessing has been bestowed upon you and the benefits of that blessing show up in some form later on. Sooner or later, if you are paying attention, you are able to look back and see that blessing has appeared in your life.

Life is a beautiful adventure, going forth unafraid in to the unknown, savoring the people you meet, the sunsets and sunrises, and everything else that you encounter along the way. Your life is more exciting that you have ever experienced it before. Face your fear and do it anyway! **F.E.A.R.** is only an acronym for *False Expectations Appearing Real*. Ghosts and goblins belong on Halloween. They don't really exist. What you are seeing is only an illusion, showing you where learning needs to take place. Love yourself! Love your life! And enjoy the journey.

There is not a moment in which His Voice fails to direct my thoughts, guide my actions and lead my feet. I am walking steadily on toward truth.

Workbook, pg. 101

We will not let the beliefs of the world tell us that what God would have us do is impossible. Instead, we will try to recognize that only what God would have us do is possible.

Workbook, pg. 71

No one is where he is by accident and chance plays no part in God's plan.

Manual for Teachers, pg. 26

Ah! Sweet Mystery
Of Life

"Ah! Sweet mystery of life, at last I've found thee.
Ah! I know at last the secret of it all.
All the longing, striving, seeking, waiting, yearning,
The burning hopes, the joys and idle tears that fall!
For 'tis love, and love alone, the world is seeking,
And it's love, and love alone, that can reply.
'Tis the answer,' tis the end and all of living,
For it is love alone that rules for aye!"
- Rida Johnson Young, librettist, **"Naughty Marietta"**

How true! Love—God—is the deepest desire of all—that for which you are looking, and that with which you looking!

Constantly search your heart. If you are not feeling loving, then you are in error and fear. Choose once again. Look for love in those places where the ego tells you that love cannot be. Look for love when your world is falling apart. Look for love when it seems that only chaos, drama, and trauma are present. Look for love when you don't have the energy.

Deep within your judgments of yourself, your fears, and your circumstances, love is, and all is well, because love cannot be lost; therefore *you* cannot be lost. Physical things and people come and go, circumstances constantly change, but love never changes and never goes away.

Your task is not to seek for love, but merely to seek and find all the barriers within yourself that you have built against it.

Text, pg. 338

Your Burden of Guilt

All blame is a waste of time. No matter how much fault you find with another, and regardless of how much you blame him, it will not change you. The only thing blame does is to keep the focus off you when you are looking for external reasons to explain your unhappiness or frustration. You may succeed in making another feel guilty about something by blaming him, but you won't succeed in changing whatever it is about you that is making you unhappy.

- Wayne Dyer

The lessons taught in *A Course in Miracles* are very practical. When you are feeling guilty, being judgmental, in pain, or fear, you are weakening yourself. The study of kinesiology is a shining example of disempowerment. The practitioner of kinesiology tests your strength as you are thinking positive thoughts or holding a substance that is good for your body, and then tests your strength again while you are holding negative thoughts or holding a substance that is not healthy for your body. Your strength is lessened when holding negative thoughts or a substance that is not healthy for your body.

You are like an iceberg, with guilt buried below the surface, the amount of guilt, of course, varies with each person. Guilt from the past, for what you did or didn't do, what you thought or didn't think, guilt from failing other people's expectations for you— parents, teachers, siblings, etc. As you bring each thought of guilt to the surface, it decreases the baggage you have been carrying, and who could run a marathon pulling 500 lbs. of baggage behind? You lose your energy, passion, and vitality to this constant weight. How much of an iceberg are you carrying? Let it go. Be constantly aware moment by moment to your ego thoughts. Cancel them immediately! Devote time each day to forgiving totally some part of your iceberg and be at peace.

The ego teaches you to attack yourself because you are guilty, and this must increase the guilt...The Holy Spirit, dispels it simply through the calm recognition that it has never been. As He looks upon the guiltless Son of God, He knows that this is true.

Text, pg. 239

Love Is What You Are

If we make our goal to live a life of compassion and unconditional love, then the world will indeed become a garden where all kinds of flowers can bloom and grow.

- Elisabeth Kubler-Ross

Define love? No, you can't define love, just like you can't define God. Anytime you try, no matter what words you use, it simply becomes a boundary, a wall. Love—it is closer than hands and feet. It is greater than your imagination can extend. It is the glue that holds the world together. It is the lubricant that keeps friction from destroying the universe. It extends inwardly and outwardly to forever and beyond. Love is natural; love is kind. Love does not judge. Love does not attack in any way, shape, or form.

Love is without condition—unconditional. Unconditional love does not bind, does not imprison, and does not restrain in any way. Unconditional love has no expectations, no requirements. When you love unconditionally, you accept the other person with all of their points, both "good" and "bad". You accept them just as they are; there is no "good" or "bad" in love. A child comes into the world loving unconditionally; they are taught to be judging and fearful.

Love is what you are; you *are* love, down to the smallest part of you. For you to be loving should be natural and easy. Give love to all who come into your presence and to all those who are far away; there is no near nor far in love. No matter how well established, hatred and fear have no power in the face of love; hatred and fear have only the power that you give them, anyway.

Love is where you came from, love from God within;
Love is where you're going, light surrounded by love.

Love yourself; love all others, no matter what their appearance or their history may be, no matter how they have treated you, no matter how real that may appear. Let go of all attack, real and imagined, justified and un-attributed. Love is the word for the day, the week, and for the rest of your life. Live it, love it, express it, and be it, now and forevermore!

Offer love, and it will come to you, because it is drawn to itself. But offer attack and love will remain hidden, for it can live only in peace.

Text, pg. 233 (paraphrased)

Nothing around you but is part of you. Look on it lovingly, and see the light of Heaven in it.

Text, pg. 486

How lovely is the world whose purpose is forgiveness of God's Son! How free from fear, how filled with blessing and with happiness!

Text, pg. 617

Steps to Awareness

"Change is certain. Peace is followed by disturbances; departure of evil men by their return. Such recurrences should not constitute occasions for sadness but realities for awareness, so that one may be happy in the interim."

- The I Ching

First, realize that this world is insane. This is a crazy, insane world that is driven by your judgments and false perceptions, your fear, and your pain. You are caught up in a lot of stinking thinking!

Second, change your mind about yourself, others, and the world in which you live. Face the insanity. Your ego does not want you to grow spiritually because its very existence is threatened by that growth. Trust that God will help you to see through the false perceptions, to release the judgments, the fear and the pain. Ask for help. The Holy Spirit was given you to offset the ego's voice in your ear. The Holy Spirit is there to take away your judgments, false perceptions, pain, and fear, and any other blockage to your growth, but you have to let go of them before He can help. You let go of one branch before you can jump to the next, and you have to let go of all branches before you can fly.

Third, realize that your ego has a function in your life. Face your fears, your ghosts, your judgments, your past, and your fears. They are lies—lies that you have told yourself, lies that others have told you, all of which you have bought into—hook, line, and sinker. They are not real—they are part of the insanity. Make a thorough list of them and embrace each one individually as you lovingly release them. Release daily. Acknowledge them and allow them to be there without resistance or resentments of any kind. You simply do not need them; they don't serve you any more. You need nothing outside of yourself—in you is where the great treasure house lies. Nothing from outside yourself can heal you or fulfill you. Your history does not make you a bad person. You are more powerful, with God on your side, than you ever dream you could be. That "hole" in you that needs filling with all the ego's stuff is nothing more than your missing conscious connection to God. Your life is the Life of God. He is nearer than hands or feet; that connection with Him can never be broken.

Fourth, rise above all perceived faults and walk a higher road. They are not true. As you walk that higher road, the ghosts may come back to haunt you again from time to time. The higher you rise, the harder that the ego fights. You may even find yourself completely caught up in them again for a while (go temporarily insane), but you can never return to where you were. You now know that you are not insane in moments like those, *merely temporarily deluded.* You are perfect, whole, and complete in truth, just as God created you; you have not changed at all. When you return to sanity, forgive yourself, and continue on. As you go through this over and over again, you develop "spiritual muscle" that makes it easier to heal your insanity and recover more easily when you stumble again.

Fifth, you eventually and gradually find yourself more peaceful (less chaotic), happier, and in great joy during *both* the "good" times and the "bad" times, knowing that, through it all, you were always on your path whether you knew it or not.

Sometimes, as you change, you find your world seemingly falling apart. An old friends' energy may not fit in your new world. Your eyes are no longer fixed merely upon the physical things of this world. You find your world rearranging itself to a new paradigm; change can be painful, not only to yourself, but to your friends and relatives. You finally realize that your life's journey has been always taking you toward a place which you never left in the first place (and never could leave), and that is the Love of God. You find new friends and new interests that serve you spiritually.

The goal is not the destination, but the journey. For example, if you are dancing, you don't usually hare a hard and fast plan to wind up the dance in a particular position with your partner nor a particular spot on the floor—you just relax and enjoy the dance. So, enjoy the dance! Have fun! Relax! Life is an adventure or it is nothing at all. The hard times, in retrospect, become the good old days, the days when you grew the most in so many ways. Look to your Angels for help and support—they come in many forms, with many different faces.

*Be comforted and feel the Holy Spirit watching over you in love
and perfect confidence in what He sees.*

Text, pg. 436

*All this beauty will rise to bless your sight as you look upon the world with
forgiving eyes. For forgiveness literally transforms vision, and lets you see
the real world reaching quietly and gently across chaos, removing all illusions
that had twisted your perception and fixed it on the past. The smallest leaf
becomes a thing of wonder, and a blade of grass a sign of God's perfection.*

Text, pg. 354

*If you are trusting in your own strength, you have every reason
to be apprehensive anxious, and fearful.*

Workbook, pg. 75

A New Way of Living

Be grateful each minute for the life God has given you, His life. Don't demean yourself or raise yourself above others, they possess the same Divine Life as you do. Be appreciative for all of the opportunities you have in this life at this time to grow spiritually through experiences whether or not they are painful. Spiritual awareness is obtained at the cost of bringing up all of the things you have hidden over the years—bringing them to the light for forgiveness and for letting go. It may be dark and murky down there, but the things that are buried in your subconscious weigh you down and hold you back. They most likely won't look nearly as bad as you were afraid they would. Things can be hidden so well that you can't remember them. They can be forgiven as well—you don't really have to know what they are. You will be able to tell when these things have left, though—you will feel so much lighter.

Rev. Dr. Kay Hunter tells her story of the time that she realized she resented a cat. It seems that many years ago, she was skipping school. She hid under the porch when she heard her mother coming. The mother cat had her kittens under the porch and her meowing led Kay's mother to the spot where Kay was hidden, and of course Kay was punished. She also tells of realizing that she still had resentments that needed to be forgiven for a girl who "did her wrong" seventy or more years ago in elementary school. It had been unconsciously weighing on her that long!

Give grateful thanksgiving to everyone and everything in your life, for the physical universe in which you live—your body, your family, your country, and your world. It may not look the way you want it to look right now, but it has manifested according to your subconscious will. As you upgrade your willingness to give and to realize that you receive in according to your giving, your physical surroundings upgrade also.

You are loved. You are loved whether you consciously realize it or not. God sends His love from your inner self, from others, and from earth itself. You are an instrument of God's Love to the extent that you allow love to flow. Bathe in the warmth of God's Love as you would bathe in the water or the Sun's light.

God does indeed love you totally—you are His Son, His Creation, in whom He is well pleased.

I was working one day and a co-worker sent a broadcast email out offering a free computer to the first person who replied. I immediately replied and received a message that I was the first to reply and would be the recipient of the computer. All of this was broadcast to the whole department. A week went by without any word. I finally emailed him about the computer—what was going on, and he said that his wife had nixed the deal, that I wasn't going to get the computer. I was very angry and embarrassed. I refused to speak to him and went to great lengths to avoid him. Finally, after I cooled down a little bit, I remembered the Course and how forgiveness might be appropriate in this situation. I no longer avoided him, even sat down to lunch at a table where he was sitting. I did not talk about the computer with him, but simply loved him for the Son of God that he was, and refused to be in anger any more. I was able to let the anger go—we didn't become best friends, you understand, but very often I was with him without any regret or upset at all.

Be forgiving and compassionate towards others who are sharing this world with you. They are giving you opportunities to practice love and forgiveness in many ways. Your family, your friends, your co-workers, the worker in the store, and the driver on the street are actually mirrors of your thoughts about yourself that you have hidden. Cast love, forgiveness, and compassion around you wherever you go and it will be returned to you. Know that the universe is not out to *get* you. It is there to *support* you.

If you only look at yourself you cannot find yourself,
because that is not what you are.

Text, pg. 42

Commitment

If you make the unconditional commitment to reach your most important goals, if the strength of your decision is sufficient, you will find the way and the power to achieve your goals.

- Robert Conklin

Commitment is the focus of one's talents, interests, goals, and dreams upon a certain outcome in his/her life. A sailor is committed to travel to a certain port. He sets his sails and rudder to move his ship in that direction. However, he is subject to activity of the winds and seas that tend to move his ship in other directions. At one point he may even find himself temporarily heading in exactly the opposite direction. He will probably have to change the settings of the sails and rudder many, many times before his ship arrives safely in port. But if he doesn't despair, if he holds faith in his ship and his compass, he will arrive.

It is the same in your life. You are subject to the powerful group thinking of your family, your local area, your nation, and your world from the time you are conceived. If you set a goal that is contrary to the thinking of your family, for example, your actions are often disapproved, frowned upon, or discounted. It may be that your actions bring pain to your mother and father—they are different from the "tradition" that has been established over the years. You also subject to your own fears of failure, disapproval, and loss. If you keep faith, hold on, persist, you will reach your goal despite this resistance.

An interesting story is that of the pig and the hen and the discussion of which is most committed to a breakfast meal. Of course the pig is, because he has to give up his life. On the other hand, the hen is, also, because she has to give up a chick. Both have great interest in whether or not the diner is a vegetarian!

The old Chinese proverb is that the journey of a thousand miles begins with a single step. The traveler must be concerned with the thousands of other steps in between the first and the last. Each step does not need to be consistent with the goal, however. The way may sometimes be lost, but regained as quickly. No matter what barriers come up, no matter what distractions appear, hold fast, think ahead, and realize that all barriers are but are challenges to be overcome.

Be vigilant only for God and His Kingdom.

Text, pg. 109

You cannot be totally committed sometimes.

Text, pg. 127

Your mind is dividing its allegiance between two kingdoms, and you are totally committed to neither. Your identification with the Kingdom is totally beyond question except by you, when you are thinking insanely. What you are is not established by your perception, and is not influenced by it at all. Perceived problems in identification at any level are not problems of fact. They are problems of understanding, since their presence implies a belief that what you are is up to you to decide. The ego believes this totally, being fully committed to it. It is not true. The ego therefore is totally committed to untruth, perceiving in total contradiction to the Holy Spirit and to the knowledge of God.

Text, pg. 125

Humankind

"Humankind has not woven the web of life. We are but one thread within it. Whatever we do to the web, we do to ourselves. All things are bound together. All things connect."

- Chief Seattle

You might ask, "How do I come to trust people and to appreciate myself?" People, in general, tend to be very fearful. You probably were conditioned during your childhood to be fearful of others because your parents wanted to protect you from harm. This may take time to overcome. Race, religion, creed or national origin is of little importance when it comes to basic human nature. In the Far East, they have the word "Namaste," which means, "The Christ in me salutes the Christ in you." If you look into another person's eyes and recognize that that human being is worthwhile, no matter what the superficial appearances might be, no matter what that person's behavior is at the time, that person will most likely acknowledge you and appreciate you. Given the opportunity, over a period of time, a bond of friendship may be formed. See the Christ in the eyes of all those you meet.

Hear the silent request for love beating deep within the hearts of every person you meet. In other words, separate the act from the actor. The act may be despicable, but the actor is a Child of God, in pain and searching for love in the best way he knows how at this time in his development. You don't have to move in with him, but you can honor his Christ nature, even though you don't see it in his behavior. The highest official and the lowest beggar, the richest man in the world and the clerk behind the courthouse desk will respond to love and a sense of humor. Animals also will respond, and studies show that plants respond, also. It just makes sense that a loving person will go through life more easily than the person with a chip on the shoulder and is angry and belligerent. Try it! As you practice it over a period of time, it can't help but pay dividends in many ways.

In everyone you see but the reflection of what you choose to have him be to you.

Text, pg. 528

God is praised whenever any mind learns to be truly helpful.

Text, pg. 71

When a brother behaves insanely, you can heal him only by perceiving the sanity in him. If you perceive his errors and accept them, you are accepting yours. If you want to give yours over to the Holy Spirit, you must do this with his.

Text, pg. 167

Developing Faith

We must not sit still and look for miracles; up and doing, and the Lord will be with thee. Prayer and pains, through faith in Christ Jesus, will do anything.

- Sir John Eliot

Acknowledge God's Activity in your life in times past. Search for success stories in your life where you stepped out on faith and God/"coincidence"/"luck" came through. For me, I set my goals the way my heart tells me to move, and then take steps to move in that direction. I don't go to a goal—live from it, live from the inspiration that it provides me. Sometimes I find walls being put up across my path that don't go down easily, Then I look for the open door that leads me around or in another direction and then take another step. This might seem wishy-washy to some, but I have faith in a perfect universe that provides all that I need to do whatever it is that my heart leads me to do. I have a condition known as reverse paranoia—believing that the Universe is out to do me Good. At one point I was transferred to Dallas, and I experienced a lot of fear and resentment. Then I found out that "wherever you go, there you are." It wasn't so bad—in fact turned out to be wonderful. I found a wonderful spiritual community and I met my wife there! Then when I was transferred to St. Louis, I had learned from the experience and there wasn't nearly as much fear involved.

To strengthen your faith, go on an internal journey to discover Who you truly are, and the deep desires of your heart. Take spiritual classes and read spiritual books and apply them to situations in your life. This study will give you clues to making decisions about what to do with your life and what God's Will is for you. The more you reach out in faith, the more faith you have. I call this doing spiritual push-ups, developing spiritual strength over a period of time, rising above the mire and murk of the insane world, all to find yourself back in it all over again. Then you rise up once again. The more you practice, the easier it becomes, and the shorter a time you spend in the muck and the mire.

You have been told that you will be fed and clothed like the birds in the fields, but that does not mean that you are entitled to have those and do nothing—sit in a cave and withdraw from the world. There is a Zen story—before enlightenment—go to well and draw water, after enlightenment, go to well and draw water. Life doesn't necessarily change drastically. It means that you ask for guidance how you can best serve God in your life and how you can give most effectively. Look for ways to give from the Abundance and Love of God within you. Have faith that "as you give, so shall you receive."

Summary. Listen and grow. Meditate and grow. Study and grow. Risk and grow. Christ has set for you the example of a life lived in faith, devotion to God, and in dedication to ministering to human need. As you search for Truth and open yourself to God's Presence in prayer and meditation, and step out on faith, you will discover more completely what God is trying to say to you. The answer is not coming from 'out there' because the answer to the prayer is in the pray-er.

And you will believe.

And you will trust.

And you will know faith.

And you will have faith.

And you will *know.*

And you will *have.*

And you will *be.*

Miracles are natural. When they do not occur something has gone wrong.

Text, pg. 3

A son of God is happy only when he knows he is with God. That is the only environment in which he will not experience strain, because that is where he belongs.

Text, pg. 136

144

Christ

Above all the grace and the gifts that Christ gives to his beloved
is that of overcoming self.

- St. Francis of Assisi

I strive to live my life as Christ lived his life. I am here to extend God's healing power to everyone I meet, to reach out to the lame and halt, just as Christ did. It seems that people who claim to be Christians so commonly ignore Christ's teachings! Christ taught love, and peace, joy, and harmony. Christ would have you love your fellowman and not judge him.

Many churches believe that they are right and other churches are wrong the way that they worship God. Religions tend to separate one group from another in competition, while spirituality draws upon that common thread that all men have in common— the presence of God within them. God is not a Baptist, nor a Methodist, nor a Catholic, nor any other denomination or sect. God can be found in all people and all religions. God can be found anywhere, not just in Church. Christ said the Kingdom of God is at hand. It is right here within your reach. You are the light of the world. Christ did not come here to be worshipped; he came to show you the way to worship God as Father. You don't need gurus to worship—not Gandhi nor Christ nor Buddha, nor anybody else. They can teach you what they saw only to a certain extent, and inspire you, but choose to assimilate their teachings in a practical way in your everyday life as best you can.

When I said, "I am with you always," I meant it literally. I am not absent to anyone in any situation. Because I am always with you, you are the way, the truth and the life. You did not make this power any more than I did. It was created to be shared.

Text, pg. 116

145

Row Your Own Boat!

A man's conscience and his judgment is the same thing; and as the judgment, so also the conscience, may be erroneous.

- Thomas Hobbes

There is only one boat that you can steer and row—it is yours. Anytime that you attempt to row someone else's boat, you usually will find yourself being resented, resisted, and attacked. Sometimes it is a nightmare, sometimes very, very nice, but nonetheless a dream. There is a story about a man who was in the doctor's office waiting for the doctor to see him. There was another man across the room who had turned his daughter over to the nurse and who looked very tense and nervous. Suddenly came a terrible scream from behind the door. The nervous man jumped up and started weeping. The other man looked at him and exclaimed, "How awful! Is that your child in there? She must be in agony! How terrible! The second man looked at him through his tears and said, "You don't understand. These tears are tears of joy! You see, my daughter has been mute all of her life. These are the first sounds she has made! Her scream was but an announcement of her voice being born. It is not terrible—it is wonderful, and I am wonder-filled!"

The first man was judging through his history what the screams and tears meant and interpreting it through his judging mind. He did not know all the facts. You cannot judge anything because you do not know all the facts. Only God can judge truly.

The miracle is means to demonstrate that all appearances can change because they are appearances, and cannot have the changelessness reality entails. The miracle attests salvation from appearances by showing they can change.

Text, pgs. 642-3

Conflict

Whenever you're in conflict with someone, there is one factor that can make the difference between damaging your relationship and deepening it. That factor is attitude.

- Timothy Bentley

Often, conflicts between persons originates because one person has not kept his agreements, not being in integrity with his word. Too often, individuals do not take their words seriously. How do you feel when someone is late? Treat others the way you would like to be treated. If you agree to meet someone, be there as closely to on time as possible. Let him know if there is a conflict or if you will be late. You *are* your word!

People in your life present their issues to you to be healed; they may seem to be in trouble. Their "story" may be devastating! People are abused in so many ways—emotionally, sexually, spiritually, physically, and so on. Their parents, peers, siblings, teachers, or family, have abused them. You don't find too many homes that are not codependent to one extent or another. Your task is to know they are not their wounds, even when they don't know. If you buy into their tragedy, if you feel pity for them, you are not helping them—you are helping to keep them in the miserable place they see themselves. Your part is not to be cold and unfeeling, either, however. Be understanding and empathetic towards their pain, but don't get caught up in it. Don't allow them to pull you down with them; you can't help them by being in the same place that they are. Although misery does love company, it only serves to keep them in their misery. If you go into a sick room or a hospital room and see a sick person, you are in the wrong place. Leave and don't come back in until you can come back in to see a person who is *not* sick. See his spiritual nature, rather than his body. Know that the Truth of him is the nature of God and therefore cannot be sick. I am not denying sickness. I am just denying that the Spirit can be sick. See the highest and best in him and he will respond. See his spiritual strength, his spiritual Truth *for* him, since he is unable to do it for himself. You will then be an uplifting force in the space and help him in his healing process.

If someone seems to be attacking you, he is acting out of fear, and it probably has more to do with him than it does with you! It is a call for love. We are like fingers of a hand, radiating from the same source, made of the same substance, like spokes of a wheel, radiating out from the center, like waves on the ocean, like rays from the sun. The wave cannot exist without the ocean and the ray cannot exist without the sun. God created one Son, expressed in many forms—in multiplicity. We are spirit having a physical experience. Humankind is a brotherhood of equals, co-creators with God of our individual worlds. Each person lives in a world of mirrors. Remain open to the movement of God through you and everyone you meet.

Look on people as the Sufi Blessing says:

"May the Blessing of God be upon you. May His Peace abide with you. May His Presence illuminate your heart, now and forevermore."

If you want peace, you must give up the idea of conflict entirely and for all time.

Text, pg. 125

God is very quiet, for there is no conflict in Him.

Text, pg. 199

There is no problem in any situation that faith will not solve... Is it not possible that all your problems have been solved, but you have removed yourself from the solution?

Text, pg. 368

Faith, Part B

"Faith is a mental attitude which is so convinced of its own idea—which so completely accepts it—that any contradiction is unthinkable and impossible".

- The Science of Mind

What do you really have faith in? Such things as: Gravity? Electricity? Doctors? Surgery? Medicine? A Band-Aid? Aspirin? True faith far surpasses such physical things.

What is faith?

- Faith is evidence of reality not yet manifested.

- Faith is believing in what is true. However, faith is more than believing or even trusting, it is knowing. Do you have sufficient faith that you can move mountains? (I consider that Jesus might have had a double meaning in mind when He made that statement—the moving of an actual mountain and/or the moving of a mountain of disbelief/group belief "problems.")

- Faith is being convinced, having evidence of unseen things.

- Faith is an intangible idea of formidable potential.

- Faith is the medium within which you manifest God.

- Faith is essential. It brings great peace into a seemingly insane and chaotic world.

Faith is more than a vague and tenuous knowing about right and wrong upon which an ethic is based or platitudes to help you get through the discomforts of life. Faith is not a cerebral exercise—it is an act of Grace. Faith is what you draw upon in times of distress, chaos, confusion, and terror, a bridge to realizing the Peace of God. Believing is not exactly the same as faith. For belief to be faith, it must light on what is true. Sometimes there's no time for evidence collection—to wait for certainty. Just have faith, like Peter walking on the water; in other words, don't think, act! God even requires you to believe in

Him when, temporarily, the evidence your eyes see looks "bad."

You whose mind is darkened by doubt and guilt, remember this: God gave the Holy Spirit to you, and gave Him the mission to remove all doubt and every trace of guilt that His dear Son has laid upon himself. It is impossible that this mission fail. Nothing can prevent what God would have accomplished from accomplishment. Whatever your reactions to the Holy Spirit's Voice may be, whatever voice you choose to listen to, whatever strange thoughts may occur to you, God's Will is done. You will find the peace in which He has established you.

Text, pg. 267

A Letter from God

God is definitely out of the closet.
- Marianne Williamson

Subject: Letter from God

My Dear Children (and believe me that's all of you):

I consider myself a pretty patient being, I mean, look at the Grand Canyon. It took millions of years to get it right. And about evolution? Boy, nothing is slower than designing that whole Darwinian thing to take place, cell by cell, and gene by gene. I've been patient through your fashions, civilizations, wars and schemes, and the countless ways you take Me for granted until you get yourself into big trouble again and again.

I want to let you know some of the things that are starting to tick me off. First of all, your religious rivalries are driving Me up a wall. Enough already!

Let's get one thing straight. These are *your* religions, not Mine. I'm the whole enchilada; I'm beyond them all. Every one of your religions claims there is only one of Me (which by the way, is absolutely true). But in the very next breath, each religion claims it's My favorite one. And each claims its bible was written personally by Me, and that all the other bible's are man-made. Oh, Me. How do I even begin to put a stop to such complicated nonsense?

Okay, listen up now. I'm you Father *and* Mother, and I *don't* play favorites among MY children. Also, I hate to break it to you, but I don't write. My longhand is awful, and I've always been more of a quote, doer end quote, anyway. So ALL of your books, including those bible's, were written by men and women. They were inspired, remarkable people, but they also made mistakes here and there. I made sure of that, so you would never trust a written word more than your own living heart.

You see, one human being to me—even a bum on the street—is worth more than all the Holy Books in the world. That's just the kind of guy I am. My Spirit is not a historical thing. It's alive right here, right now, as fresh as your next breath. Holy books and religious rites are sacred and powerful, but not more so than the least of you. They were only meant to steer you in the right direction, not to keep you arguing with each other, and certainly not to keep you from trusting your own personal connection with Me.

Which brings Me to My next point about your nonsense. You act like I need you and your religions to stick up for Me or quote, win souls end quote for My sake Please, don't do Me any favors. I can stand quite well on my own, thank you. I don't need you to defend Me, and I don't need constant credit, I just want you to be good to each other.

And another thing: I don't get all worked up over money or politics, so stop dragging My name into your dramas. For example, I swear to Me that I never threatened Oral Roberts. I never rode in any of Rajneesh's Rolls Royce's. I never told Pat Robertson to run for President, and I've never EVER had a conversation with Jimmy Bakker, Jerry Falwell, or Jimmy Swaggart! Of course, come Judgment Day, I certainly intend to. The thing is, I want you to stop thinking of religion as some sort of loyalty pledge to Me. The true purpose of your religions is so you can become more aware of ME, not the other way around. Believe Me, I know you already. I know what's in each of your hearts, and I love you with no strings attached. Lighten up and enjoy Me. That's what religion is best for you. What you seem to forget is how mysterious I am. You look at the petty differences in your Scriptures and say, & quote, well, if THIS is the truth, then THAT can't be! end quote; But instead of trying to figure out my Paradoxes and Unfathomable Nature—which by the way, you NEVER will—why not open your hearts to the simple common threads in all religions? You know what I am talking about:

Love and respect everyone.

Be kind, even when life is scary or confusing, take courage and be good of cheer, for I am always with you.

Learn how to be quiet, so you can hear my small still voice (I don't like to shout).

Leave the world a better place by living your life with dignity and gracefulness, for you are My Own Child.

Hold back Nothing from life, for the parts of you that can dies surely will, and the parts that can't won't.

So don't worry, be happy (I stole that last line from Bobby

McFerrin, but Who do you think gave it to him in the first place?)

Simple stuff. Why do you keep making it so complicated? It's like you're always looking for an excuse to be upset? And I'm very tired of being your main excuse. Do you think I care whether you call Me Yahweh, Jehovah, Allah, Wakantonka, Brahma, Father, Mother or even the Void of Nirvana? Do you think I care which of My special children you feel closest to—Jesus, Mary, Buddha, Krishna, Mohammed, or any of the others? You can call Me and My Special Ones any name you choose, if only you would go about My business of loving one another as I love you. How can you keep neglecting something so simple? I'm not telling you to abandon your religions. Enjoy your religions, honor them, learn from them, just as you should enjoy, honor, and learn from your parents. But do you walk around telling everyone that your parents are better than theirs? Your religion, like your parents, may always have the most special place in your heart, I don't mind that at all. And I don't want you to combine all the Great Traditions in One Big Mess.

Each religion is unique for a reason.

Each has a unique style so that people can find the best path for themselves.

But My Special Children—the ones that your religions revolve around—all live in the same place (My heart) and they get along perfectly, I assure you.

The clergy must stop creating a myth of sibling rivalry where there is none. My blessed children of Earth, the world had grown too small for your pervasive religious bigotry's and confusion. Air travel, satellite dishes, telephones, fax machines, rock concerts, diseases, and mutual needs and concerns connect the whole planet. Get with the program!

If you really want to help then commit yourself to figuring out how to feed your hungry, clothe your naked, protect your abused, and shelter your poor. And just as importantly, make your own everyday life a shining example of kindness and good humor.

I've given you all the resources you need, if only you abandon your fear of each other and begin living, loving, and laughing together.

Finally, My Children everywhere, when you think of the life of Jesus and the fearlessness with which He chose to live and die. As I love Him, so do I love each one of you. I'm not really ticked off, I just wanted to grab your attention because I hate to see you suffer. But I gave you free will.

I just want you to be happy. God never gives you what you are not ready to accept.

Always.

Trust in Me

Your One and Only,

God

- From email—author unknown

There is no substitute for truth. And truth will make this plain to you as you are brought into the place where you must meet with truth. And there you must be led, through gentle understanding which can lead you nowhere else. Where God is, there are you. Such is the truth.

Text, pg. 290

Look with peace upon your brothers, and God will come rushing into your heart in gratitude for your gift to Him.

Text, pg. 191

The Silent Prayer
From Tobias, channeled by
Geoffrey Hoppe

If I could define enlightenment briefly I would say it is
"the quiet acceptance of what is."

\- Wayne Dyer

The Silent Prayer is an acknowledgement of All That Is. In this prayer, I know that every prayer I have ever voiced is heard by Spirit, and that Spirit has given unto me all that I have asked for. It is an acknowledgement that my soul is complete in the love and grace of God. It is an acknowledgement of my total state of perfection and Is-ness. All that I desire, all that I wish to co-create, is already within my reality. I call this the Silent Prayer because I know that my Being is already fulfilled. There is no need to ask for anything of Spirit, because it has already been given.

In my heart, I accept my perfect Being.
I accept that the joy that I have intended is already in my life.
I accept that love I have prayed for is already within me.
I accept that the peace I have asked for is already my reality.
I accept that the abundance I have sought already fills my life.

In my truth, I accept my perfect Being.
I take responsibility for my own creations,
And all things that are within my life.
I acknowledge the power of Spirit that is within me,
And know that all things are as they should be.

In my wisdom, I accept my perfect Being.
My lessons have been carefully chosen by my Self,
And now I walk through them in full experience.
My path takes me on a sacred journey with divine purpose.
My experiences become part of All That Is.

In my knowingness, I accept my perfect Being.

In this moment, I sit in my golden chair
And know that I Am an angel of light.
I look upon the golden tray—the gift of Spirit -
And know that all of my desires already have been fulfilled.
In love for my Self, I accept my perfect Being.
I cast no judgment or burdens upon my Self.
I accept that everything in my past was given in love.
I accept that everything in this moment comes from love.
I accept that everything in my future will result in greater love.

In my Being, I accept my perfection.
And so it is.

From website **http://www.crimsoncircle.com**

It is quite possible to reach God. In fact, it is very easy, because it is the most natural thing in the world. You might say that it is the only natural thing in the world. The way will open, if you believe that it is possible...You can indeed laugh at fear thoughts, remembering that God is with you wherever you go.

Workbook, pg. 64

God is my strength. Vision is His gift...God is my Source.
I cannot see apart from Him.

Workbook, pgs. 65-67

Pray Not

I pray without ceasing now. My personal prayer is:
Make me an instrument which only truth can speak.

- Peace Pilgrim

Pray not for completion, but to realize you were never separated in the first place and that you could never be separated from other people or from God.

Pray not for love, because you *are* love. God created you in the image of Himself and God is Love. Find that love for yourself and others right there in your own heart.

Pray not for peace, because peace is already in you. It comes alive in your thoughts, in your reaction to stimuli, and in your decision to be peaceful. It is not the problem that is the problem; it is your reaction to the problem.

Pray not for power, because God created you powerful and you have given away your power to the insane thinking and motivations of the world. You already are power-filled.

Pray not for forgiveness. God has not condemned you. You have condemned you. Forgive yourself for your failures and your errors. You are not a sinner.

Pray saying "Thy Will be done, God! God is just. God's Grace is upon you. God works in mysterious ways, but there is always a blessing in every thing that happens to you. There was a gay couple who spoke in a church about the blessings at AIDS had been in their lives. Have faith in His Divine Right Action through situations, people, and events in your life. Where one door closes, another opens.

It takes great learning to understand that all things, events, encounters and circumstances are helpful.

Manual for Teachers, pg. 10

Acting On Your Faith

"If God is calling you to action, follow the Law of Compassion. Jesus gave us the supreme demand, "Be merciful, even as our Father is merciful."

- Luke 6:36

Whenever you are confronted with a human being in need, you can be sure that the call of God is there for you to do whatever you can to help, even though this may be simply opening your heart in love and compassion while keeping your mouth shut.

If you feel in your heart a call, don't hang up! I was in meditation, rising higher and higher, reaching out, just about there, and then the ego kicked in and destroyed the image. The ego had hung up the line; fear shut down the line. The message from God may come in many ways—via men or women who are acting as Angels in your life in some way or other, and many other ways. If you, like Abraham in the Bible, show that you are willing to do the task (sacrificing his son), it usually won't be necessary for you to do it. Once you have the message, the next challenge is to be open and receptive to what God is trying to say to you, to accept the message, to have *faith* in God and *faith* in the message.

Trust would settle every problem now!

Text, pg. 55

Put all your faith in the Love of God within you; eternal, changeless and forever unfailing. This is the answer to whatever confronts you today.

Workbook pg. 79

Send Your Light

He that has light within his own clear breast may sit in the center,
and enjoy bright day: But he that hides a dark soul and foul
thoughts benighted walks under the mid-day sun.

- John Milton

Who are you? Really? I cannot remind you too often that you are a Child of God, a Being of Light! You are Spirit experiencing a human, physical condition. You are so much more than you have been pretending to be. You are a star, shining in the darkness. Your light blesses all that you are, all that you do, and all the world. Sense the magnificent light of your being radiating from you right now. Allow that pure energy awareness to surround and penetrate your body, healing the dark places and revealing yourself to you in an even greater awareness. Clean out the cobwebs in your thinking and logical pathways with this light. Remove judgments of yourself with it.

Now, send this light into your past, erasing the painful history of your family, of your past lives, of past and present suffering.

Cast this light far and wide into the world, blessing with deepest compassion all those in fear and pain, those on battlefields, those in abusive situations, those confused and lost individuals in all places.

Bless with your light those in positions of office and position, the leaders. Your light is powerful, dear ones. Let it shine!

When you are going on a trip, whether it be long or short, cast the beautiful light of your understanding along the path and upon the destination, knowing that *all* things work together for good in those and all places.

Now, send your light into your relationships, near and far, bringing love to the surface and burying old resentments, grudges, and judgments. Send it into the workplace, knowing that perfect activity takes place there right now.

Know that you are the light of the world and a power-filled man/woman in all ways, in all times, and in all things. You are an angel, beautiful, and glorious. May your day be filled with miracles in all things and in all ways.

Child of light, you know not that the light is in you. Yet you will find it through its witnesses, for having given light to them they will return it. Each one you see in light brings your light closer to your awareness. Love always leads to love.

Text pg. 252

In this world you can become a spotless mirror, in which the Holiness of your Creator shines forth from you to all around you. You can reflect Heaven here. Yet no reflections of the images of other gods must dim the mirror that would hold God's reflection in it. Earth can reflect Heaven or hell; God or the ego. You need but leave the mirror clean and clear of all the images of hidden darkness you have drawn upon it. God will shine upon it of Himself. Only the clear reflection of Himself can be perceived upon it.

Text, pg. 292

The World Is Unfair

It is only shallow people who do not judge by appearances. The true mystery of the world is the visible, not the invisible.

- Oscar Wilde

How many times each day, each week, each year, do you have the opportunity to feel unfairly treated? Did a car cut you off on the highway? Did you get a ticket for speeding? Did a tree fall on your house? Did a loved one do you wrong? Did your car fail to start? Did the government "rob" your pocket? Events such as these (and even more drastic and far-reaching events) give you the opportunity to learn, rather than to feel that the world is unfair. The truth is that the world is unfair! It wasn't set up to treat everyone exactly the way that they wish. You must take the responsibility for your world and the way that your thoughts impact it. The opportunity is for you to learn how to change your thinking and change your world. Also, when the world does not do as you wish, you can learn to not react to the world. Your reactions compound the problem, so just relax, let go, and let God.

The world is too much with you, waking and sleeping. Take some time today to be at peace, to be free of the world, to go inside and commune with God—not to tell Him what you want or what to do, but to let Him guide you and love you through it all.

The little problems that you keep and hide become your secret sins, because you did not choose to let them be removed for you. And so they gather dust and grow, until they cover everything that you perceive and leave you fair to no one.

Text, pg. 540

161

Practicing the Presence
Inspired by the book of the same name
by Joel S. Goldsmith

*I was frustrated out of my mind, trying to figure out the will of God.
I was doing everything but getting into the presence of God
and asking Him to show me.*

- Paul Little

What happens when you practice the Presence? You become a
thinner and thinner curtain between the Infinite outside
and the Infinite inside, allowing Spirit to circulate constantly
between the two. You become nonjudgmental, light, harmonious,
forgiving, happy, laughing, bright, non-competitive, loving, fair,
honest, considerate, open, flexible, faithful, at peace, thankful,
generous, and helpful. You realize that you are innocent, safe,
abundant, and blessed. You are peaceful when your mind is
stayed on Him. You are in the world, but not of it. You become
Christ washing dishes, Christ walking your dog, Christ in the
meeting at the office, doing everything as the Christ. You believe
in the perfection of the universe, that the universe is out to do
you good. You find that you would rather be kind than to be right.
You recognize that of your self you can do nothing (except find
misery and pain). You realize that with God uppermost in your
heart you have it all—with the mightiest Power in the universe
allowed to guide and to protect you.

*Only God's Comforter can comfort you. In the quiet of His temple, He waits
to give you the peace that is yours. Give His peace, that you may enter the
temple and find it waiting for you. But be holy in the Presence of God, or
you will not know that you are there.*

Text, pg. 200

The Man in the Cage

*Many people are in a rut and a rut is nothing but a grave—
with both ends kicked out.*

- Vance Havner

There is a man, a man locked deeply into a rut, a rut so deep that he is trapped, imprisoned. He is so blinded by his misperceptions that he literally cannot see a way out even though it is right in front of him. His mind is closed. His eyes are closed. His heart is closed. He is alive, but not fully alive. He is a walking, talking robot. The great paradox, or lie, is that the bars are really not there, that the walls are really not there. To the perception they seem to be real, but they are not there in truth—they are illusions. He has lied to himself. Others have lied to him. He has bought into the lie all the way. It has become his life. The thought of being outside the cage, seemingly all alone, is really frightening. However, he is never really alone. There are people and organizations ready and willing to help, both physically and spiritually.

What if all people had open minds and open hearts towards their fellow men? What if all people refrained from judging and categorizing, lumping together? What if all the prejudices and categories suddenly disappeared somehow? All of the "small" prejudices insidiously and unfairly contribute to the imprisonment of people in special cages, locked in—their children also locked in, and their children's children. They sit there in their cage; sometimes a dream of freedom rises in their hearts, only to be denied as even a possibility. The people in the cages have the opportunity to take responsibility for buying into the prison that others helped to build for them. They were not forced into these cages—their parents, siblings, peers, and teachers helped to prepare the cages for them. There are different kinds of cages; some are cruel and hard, while some are soft and comfortable. A person can be powerful in many areas of his life and yet be limited in another.

Another kind of cage that people find themselves in is the "waiting" cage—that is, enduring the present while waiting for the future, i.e., the children to grow up, retirement, a better job, for the "right" time, for more time. They spend their time regretting the past, which is gone—nothing can be changed there—and anticipating the future. They judge themselves for actions and mistakes in their past and pull themselves down into the mud. They look to the physical world for nurturing rather than from within themselves, not realizing that there is no true happiness in things material. They are totally unable to see that all they really have is right now, the present time, in which to initiate positive changes to their future, to set goals and to step toward accomplishing their dreams and ambitions.

For every example of people who broke out of their cages against great odds (Martin Luther King, Jr., Helen Keller, and Mahatma Ghandi) there are billions of others who either languished or are languishing in cages deep or shallow. One may have a specific interest and out of that interest, develop his mental faculties more than another person. A brain surgeon, for example, is not smarter than other people; his interest was in that direction and he simply applied his intelligence and developed special abilities. The huge majority of people are equal in innate abilities and strengths. Often, a disability becomes strength and an advantage because the person who has it becomes stronger by overcoming it. Jesus, Buddha, King, and Gandhi were not special, they were not greater than their parents, their siblings, and their peers—they simply made the great realization that they were free to live life differently, to see life differently, to experience life differently. They dreamed great dreams, applied themselves, and made them come true. They rose above their fears and the fears of others. The bars in their cages were not any less "real"—they were forged with their own hands from the raw materials provided by others' prejudices and judgments, but they broke through them.

The cultural flow is strong. It is hypnotizing as it proclaims your weakness and sinful nature. It is easy to deny one's own strengths and intuition and resist change. Some people would rather die than change, and often do just exactly that. Safety is found even though it is uncomfortable; safety is often valued above comfort. For example, the abused wife, seeing no way out, stays in the safety of the home even though it wounds her and can eventually kill her. "This is the way things are" is a mentality that enables one to defy even looking at doing things differently, experimenting with it, or even thinking about it. It is the easy way out to blame someone else for their misery and their cage. It signifies a sense of inevitability and resignation. They tolerate things, people, and situations that they don't like in order to escape the pain of breaking out of their comfort zone. Only when things get so bad they can't stand them anymore do they desperately thrash out or even commit suicide to escape.

Are you in a cage? Are you trapped, alone, and lost? If you find yourself lost in any kind of a dark place in your life, realize that you are greater than you think, much greater and more powerful than you could ever imagine. You can accomplish miracles by simply changing your mind, by thinking positively, and by uniting yourself with God! One man together with Spirit can face anyone and anything. One man together with Spirit can break free. One man with Spirit can change the world! You can break out of the chains, and dissolve the bars. Even if the bars and chains are physically real, when you align yourself with Spirit, you can be free even while in prison, because freedom is not in the physical— it is in the mind. One man, aligned with Spirit, can awaken others to his Truth and be set free from the darkness that encompasses him. Remember that no matter where you are and whatever is going on, you are at choice. Put your self in the Hands of God, have faith in His Love and His Strength in you, or go on down the same miserable road over and over again. Awaken to Him now and save your life.

The Holy Spirit's teaching takes only one direction and has only one goal; His direction is freedom and His goal is God.

Text, pg. 141

I have invented the world I see. I made up the prison in which I see myself. All I need do is recognize this and I am free. I have deluded myself into believing it is possible to imprison the Son of God. I was bitterly mistaken in this belief, which I no longer want. The Son of God must be forever free.

Text, pg. 94

About the Author

I have been studying metaphysical principles and facilitating study groups in *A Course in Miracles* for close to twenty years. This book is taken from my teaching notes and material that has inspired me through the years. I am an author, poet, and artist. My poetry is sprinkled throughout this document. I wrote, printed, published, and distributed my first book, *A Course in Miracles in a Nutshell* in 1997. That volume, in a new, expanded Second Edition, became the first in a trilogy of *"Nutshell"* volumes, all available now. The other two books are:

This book, *A Course in Miracles in a Nutshell Book Two: Inspirational Messages from the Heart*
(ISBN 0-9777219-1-4, $14.00, Transformation Publications, Mesa AZ) and
A Course in Miracles in a Nutshell Book Three: More Inspirational Messages from the Heart
(ISBN 0-9777219-2-2, $14.00, Transformation Publications, Mesa AZ).

All of my books are available in bookstores, at many online bookstores such as Amazon.com, and direct from my personal website, http://www.budmorris.com.

My goal in life is to remember more of my spiritual truth each day and to teach that truth to everyone I meet; i.e., to unconditionally love everyone I encounter and to help heal the insanity of this world through that unconditional love. I seek each day to be continually practicing the Presence of God and to pray unceasingly, at the same time carrying on a life filled with activities.

Printed in the United States
99609LV00014B/160-165/A